Puppy Training

The Beginner's Guide to Training a Puppy with Dog Training Basics: Includes Potty Training for Puppy and The Art of Raising a Puppy with Positive Puppy Training

Corinne Elliott

form the information ultimately takes. This includes copied versions of the work, both physical, digital, and audio unless express consent of the Publisher is provided beforehand. Any additional rights reserved.

Furthermore, the information that can be found within the pages described forthwith shall be considered both accurate and truthful when it comes to the recounting of facts. As such, any use, correct or incorrect, of the provided information will render the Publisher free of responsibility as to the actions taken outside of their direct purview. Regardless, there are zero scenarios where the original author or the Publisher can be deemed liable in any fashion for any damages or hardships that may result from any of the information discussed herein.

Additionally, the information in the following pages is intended only for informational purposes and should thus be thought of as universal. As befitting its nature, it is presented without assurance regarding its prolonged validity or interim quality. Trademarks that are mentioned are done without written consent and can in no way be considered an endorsement from the trademark holder.

Some may believe that potty training is as simple as only having the dog on a daily routine of feeding, drinking, and potty-outs where she is carried out every few hours. Or they believe after only a week or two, the dog should be fully housetrained. That may be so for certain precocious pups; however, other puppies who are put to such a loose, abbreviated potty regimen are only slightly housetrained, or have potty accidents for months.

These little Rovers know that potting out is fine, but they don't get it's out of limits inside.In fact, after a lengthy play or workout session, they may also come inside and relieve themselves on your luxurious carpet.

That's because potty training is not just about where to go to the school. It's all about making clear that other places are unacceptable, so potting is a routine even in the right places.

Since the moment you get it home you will need to start teaching your dog to start house cleaning. Puppies start learning from birth and successful breeders quickly start treating and socializing. Any training can start as soon as the puppy is able to open its eyes and walk. Young puppies have limited periods of concentration but you can expect them to start practicing basic obedience commands like "down," "down," and "stop," as soon as 7 to 8 weeks old.

Traditionally, intensive dog discipline was postponed until about 6 months. This juvenile period is really a really poor time to get going. The dog learns from any practice and avoiding teaching ensures missed opportunities for the dog to know how you want to act like him.

The dog starts to solidify adult behavioral patterns during the developmental stage, and develops through cycles of anxiety. Behaviors acquired during puppyhood may need to adjust. Moreover, something that has already been mastered or poorly qualified will need to be removed and re-taken. Puppies can learn much from an early age.
Use approaches that focus on positive reinforcement and supportive coaching while training is begun at 7 to 8 weeks of age, puppies have short attention spans, and training sessions should be brief, but should take place every day.

Using a method called food-lure teaching, puppies can be trained to "down," "down," and "stand" They use nutritional treats to entice the canine to follow his paws in the proper "down," "down," "stand," and "wait" poses. Small pieces of food or a favorite pet can be used to inspire the puppy to do most of the activities. If the reward is enticing enough, the puppy may be encouraged to offer the desired response by presenting the reward to the puppy, issuing an order, and shifting the reward to get the desired response.

For starters, food placed over the puppy's nose and moved slowly backwards should receive a 'down' response; food pulled down to the ground should receive a 'down' response; food brought back up should receive a 'stand' response; food kept at a distance should receive a 'come' response; and food held at the knee as you walk should get the puppy to 'heel or' jump.

The puppy would quickly learn the meaning of each order by combining a command phrase or word with each move, and providing the reward for each appropriate response.
Ideally you will give the term of order once and then use your food to push your puppy into positions.

Once the puppy has completed the job, put in overt reinforcement and affectionate hug, regarded as secondary reinforce, If the puppy does not follow on the first order automatically, then you will possibly move a little too quickly. If you continue to repeat the order, the puppy will understand that it requires multiple repetitions before it has to comply. Having a leash tied will help if the dog doesn't comply to get an immediate response.

Mind your puppy doesn't know the meaning of the word, early in training. Therefore you could teach your dog just as quickly to sit with the word bananas (or sit in any other language) as you could with the word stop. The trick is to connect the term to the practice of putting the hind end on the surface, in this case "sit."

At first you'll let the puppy see the food in your pocket, so you'll get her attention and use it to direct her into position. You can start hiding the food in your hand as your puppy begins to respond more readily, but send the order and repeat the gesture or signal she's learned to obey. The puppy will quickly come to expect the reward every time she carries out the mission. Signal and give the order instead, but when she carries out the task, simply reward it with encouragement and give the puppy an affectionate hug. First, you should start changing pace, celebrating "good dog" and maybe patting each time, then occasionally offering the food, maybe every 3 or 4 days. The puppy will respond in time to either the hand signal or the order.

The words "good dog" and the affectionate touch become secondary reinforcers over time. Because in the past they were combined with food, they take on more meaning and become self-reinforced. It is necessary to use secondary motivation, because when you need your pet to comply, you won't always have food with you. Additionally, if you depend on food to get your dog to do it, you'll have a puppy that will only do the job when you're getting a treat.

Start at first training throughout the day, with a number of family members, in specified sessions. The bonuses for those training sessions should be saved. You should however start asking the dog to perform the tasks at other times over time. You don't actually have to practice each day in a fixed session. Instead, combine those activities all day long. At least 15 minutes of exercise each day is one goal to aim for.

These can vary throughout the day to be short 5 minute sessions. Seek to have your puppy remind all family members to do those things. Keep in mind trying to train in every room in your home. You want your dog to "sit down," "lie down" and "wait" everywhere, not just at the training site. Train wherever you want your puppy to behave in the future, and feel comfortable and relaxed.

Use these fitness exercises as you incorporate your puppy into your life. For examples, remind your puppy to "sit" before you get their milk, "sit" before you let her in or out of the room, and "sit" before you pet her. These are moments when you want something from your dog and are more likely to obey. In this way, you train your dog all the time, all day long and also set consistent rules and procedures for encounters to make the dog understand who manages the tools.

Training the puppy before having every need demanded helps to avoid problems. Sitting your puppy before getting a meal or reward avoids begging, whereas telling your dog to sit before opening the door can prevent the door from jumping or running out. Be imaginative. Be innovative.

When you have an adult dog, the time that you spent raising your puppy now pays off. To have a well-trained dog, you need to dedicate yourself for the first year of your puppy's life and practice the training exercises on almost a daily basis. The more you train and supervise your dog, the less opportunity it has to indulge in unethical behavior. The dogs do not teach themselves, they will behave like puppies when left to choose their actions.

Training will start with a few disruptions in a quiet environment. The reward selected should be highly motivating, so that the puppy is fully focused on the trainer and the reward. Although a small meal reward generally works well, it may be more tempting to have a favorite toy or a special dog treat.

Training the puppy just before a planned mealtime when it's at its hungryest might also be beneficial.

With troublesome or headstrong puppies, having a leash attached and using a head collar for extra supervision is the best way to ensure the puppy demonstrates the desired behavior and respond appropriately to the order. In this way, if it doesn't comply automatically, you will push the puppy into the correct response, and the strain can be released as soon as the desired response is met.
Socialization will start as soon as you get your puppy and this often means at age 7 weeks.

Puppies generally accept new people, other species and introduce new circumstances during the time of socialization which takes place between the ages of 7 and 14 to 16 weeks. This era provides an opportunity for a multitude of introductions that will provide a lifetime of positive memories. During this time, puppies are enthusiastic, exploratory and uninhibited and it is important to take advantage of that enthusiasm.

Make sure your puppy is safe during this time and make sure all the encounters are constructive, enjoyable and not evoking terror.
There is a regular, natural cycle of fear that begins at about 14 to 16 weeks. A puppy may become wary and cautious of new individuals, species or experiences during this time. That is a normal process of adaptation. Look closely at the dog for signs of anxiety (cowering, urinating, and rejecting food treats). During this developmental phase stop pressuring or upsetting the puppy

With these few simple steps, pet owners who are novices at training will launch a training programme. It takes consistency, patience and perseverance for the puppy to respond to commands in a variety of situations with predictability and durability. Consider only those classes which use constructive techniques in teaching.

A training class, however, performs a great many purposes. Trainers will highlight techniques and help guide you through the training phase. They can help educate you about issues with puppy training, and can help you progress your preparation to more challenging workouts. In a group situation the puppy should know, with some real life distractions. So, given human nature, if they don't want to be behind by the next class, the pet owner who takes his or her dog to a puppy class will be required to train (do their homework) during the week. Finally, a training course is a good place to meet and chat with other new puppy owners and see how all the puppies are doing.

There are a few things you need to get ready before your new puppy or dog arrives in to make sure they're relaxed and content in their new home.

Food and water bowls Prefer food and water bowls with heavy-bottomed ceramic or stainless steel. Plastic containers are likely to end up as chew toys, and tooth marks can become a refuge for bacteria, destroying teeth and gums. Your dog (and you) will therefore find it difficult to tip over a large bowl through an mistake.

By rule, all dogs must wear a tag on their collar which indicates the name and address of their owner. And adding your phone number is a smart idea too. Order a tag online or at the nearest pet store.

The use of micro-chipping because collars can fall off or break: it's fast, painless, permanent and reliable. Ask the vet to implant the tag, and if the puppy or child or horse is gone, you'll have a much better chance of being reunited. Check with the breeder or rescue home to see if the puppy or dog has already been micro-chipped, and ask them how to attach the chip to your address.

Anything to chew on: Dogs like to chew and a teething puppy or dog can eat something that they can get inside their jaws. And if you want to cover your boots, shoes and couch, give your puppy or dog a set of chews to test their teeth on instead. Only make sure they're non-toxic, long-lasting and not too harsh on puppy or dog teeth. And never leave your puppy or dog alone with something that could scare them, crack or electrocute them in their head.

There is an incredible range of dog toys out there – take a look at your nearest pet store or go online: you'll find healthy hoops, sticks, slings, tugs and frisbees made from leather. They are all built to make your sessions of playing and training more enjoyable-for you and your puppy.

Grooming kit It's not just about untangling their hair and making them look good for your puppy or dog, grooming is a bonding activity that encourages them to be back with their family. To pick up a comb or a towel, visit your pet store and schedule routine grooming sessions. Different coats can need specific brushes — inquire for advice from the pet shop staff, the breeder of your puppy or dog or other owners of dogs like yours.

You will still need to trim the dog's nails and periodically give them a wash – so it's worth picking up a pair of nail clippers and a dog-friendly shampoo as well.

Stair gates Steps, balconies and ponds will all be out of reach for a curious puppy or dog-so a carefully positioned baby staircase gate should do the trick if you're not there to supervise. Often, a gate will help shield your furniture and belongings from the unstopable chewing behavior of your puppy or dog.

Using a crate to carry your puppy or dog home in you might have been given a traveling crate. And as long as the crate is big enough for your puppy or dog to move in easily, it is also ideal for indoor use. Dogs tend to go to the bathroom in their own bed but in the first few weeks as the puppy or dog transitions to their new schedule, a crate is a perfect bathroom-training help. You can also use it to take them to exploring new sights and sounds in the vehicle. Put the puppy or dog to bed in their cage at night so they won't urinate or defaecate on the floor as long as you let them out at appropriate times.

First meal from your dog Arrival at their new home would be a big change for your dog. And one of the nicest things you can do is give them a cup of the same meal they're used to eating. This is going to make your dog feel comfortable and safe.

You should then determine what meal you'd like to give them afterwards. When you want to change the diet for dogs, make sure you slowly wean over 5-7 days by combining the fresh food in with the old one. It is essential to provide a full and healthy dog food suitable for the age and lifestyle of the dogs.

Collars and leads come with a wide selection of fabrics. Nylon or flexible soft leather collars are recommended because they can grow together with your puppy or dog. Change the loop, and you can place a few fingers between the collar and the neck of your puppy or dog easily. Check the fit regularly; you'll be shocked at how quickly they develop.

When you have a very little dog, such as a miniature terrier or a toy breed, you can consider having a leash – it makes it easier to cover fragile necks. (Remember to check that your puppy or dog is still sporting an ID tag.) Your puppy or dog's first visit to the vet Ask nearby dog owners to suggest a vet, or use our vet-finder app to locate a local service, take them for a walk until your dog's used to you and their new home. You will need to think about worming, vaccines, micro-chipping and neutering, in addition to a general check-up.

Carry along some toys and make the dog's big mess. A ride to the vet's might be fun for your dog with the right vet service and a good mindset, rather than terrifying.

Pet insurance: You can always have a chat about medical expenses and health benefits with the doctor. Think about what amount of protection you need, compare rates, and question insurers before you sign up to a contract about their claims process.

Bringing home a puppy

Puppies are bringing joy, warmth and lots of affection to a household and some even believe that without a puppy, no family is growing. Children learn commitment lessons with a dog, and the inevitable joy as they grow up together warms the spirit. Puppies grow their own personalities which often parallels his family's in some way. Who would resist possessing a little fuzzy bundle of joy?

Consider all that will be involved and the burden associated with owning a dog for 12 to 15 years when agreeing to purchase a puppy. The budgetary expense of owning a dog is considerable, with vet bills, dog food, bedding and toys particularly in the first year. Who should spend time with your new family member and look after him while you're gone because you always have long working hours or holidays? Only once you have thoroughly acknowledged this huge investment can you go out hunting for a dog, because there are so few people who can walk away until they fall in love with those big brown eyes.

There are plenty of possible dangers left around your house that might cause your puppy issues. Puppies are fun and adventurous animals who tend to chew on their fresh teeth and since they are tiny they can sneak into places you haven't even heard of.

Make sure the cleaners and detergents are put away securely, and the soap cakes are not in a position that your dog can get his teeth on. Don't leave plastic bags lying around that he can get tangled in and make sure small items like sewing machines and toys are not left on tables or cupboards at low level. Hold the toilet lid shut to deter the dog from jumping in the tub and eating. The lid can collapse and injure or trap him, and the cleaners and blocks in the bowls are poisonous to animals.

Houseplants can be both toxic and enticing to puppies. Remove all houseplants, or growing them beyond the grasp of your puppy in hanging baskets.

There are also risks in the garage as certain contaminants are left on the field or put at low level. Rat poison, anti-freeze, mothballs, fertilizers and insecticides in particular are all attractive to puppies because they can all prove lethal. Don't presume that this is only because the garage is closed and the puppy is free. Spend some time tidying things up and putting all the hazardous substances out of sight of the puppy.

It is important to "kitten-proof" the house when taking a curious kitten home to ensure it's healthy. Keep out of reach small things such as rubber bands, buttons and beads and be mindful that certain indoor chemicals and plants are potentially toxic to kittens.

Get down low and search behind cabinets or under sofas for any nooks and crannies the kitten may like to try. Stop these with a cardboard or add a double-sided tape, as kittens do not like the sticky paper. Cut from the shelf hanging strings and delicate ornaments, and still shut drawers and doors to the cupboard.

Dog's First Night

When your dog gets to his new home first, take him to his bathroom area and let him wander around for a while. Then, placed him for some quiet time inside his crate, there he'll be comfortable and will look at his new world without getting threatened by other people or other dogs.

Hold the dog in his cage by your side at night for the first week or two. He'll be comfortable in his own environment and you'll be able to relax in the assurance he's not getting up to mischief. Give him a chew toy and a comfortable smelling towel or blanket, and hang your arm over the bed every now and then so that he can sniff and lick your fingers before he sleeps.

Offer him a night light, and a ticking clock or soothing music, if your puppy sleeps in another room. He's likely to weep the first hour, because he missed his family.

Many puppies would need to be brought outdoors at night, and early in the morning again. Set the alarm, if possible, so that you wake up while encouraging the puppy to know the regular night time toilet and the the occurrence of soiling the bedding.

Socializing

Socializing is the period during which a puppy establishes relationships in her community with other people and animals which helps her to get used to household sounds which things like vacuum cleaners, music and car ride. Once you puppy have been vaccinated and are accustomed to walking on a leash, place him in several different scenarios and expose him to other animals (including cats, rabbits, chickens, and guinea pigs) and ensure sure all the animals are healthy. Visit beaches, lakes and festivals and even send him to a Great Pets and Gardens shop where he'll be spoiled rotten and learn to be in a new setting without being timid or scared.

Housetraining

Have a place outside where you can go to the bathroom and show your dog the right way to relieve himself. Attach his lead onto his collar and send him to the place using a "go potty" or "go bathroom" order. Repeat it often until the puppy relieves himself and then thank him for doing as you asked. It may take a bit of time so don't get upset or angry.

Take the puppy back inside for food and drink, and take him outside again to repeat the process about 15 minutes after he has finished feeding. During a meal always take the puppy to his bathroom spot before he himself starts going there.

And well-trained dogs are having injuries. Clean the place with a neutralizer pet odor and the dog would not be tempted to go back there.

If housetraining continues to be tough, a potential explanation is that so much independence has been granted to the puppy so early and so you need to go back to the training phase. When the puppy stains his crate at night, withdraw the food and water because it may load up on it and be compelled to clean itself even though it doesn't want to. A change of diet, late-night snacks and poor exercise will lead to injuries too.

Feeding

Puppies are very busy and are growing quickly and they eat up a lot of energy. It is necessary to serve them foods that are specially designed to provide a healthy and full diet that fits their stage of living. Once you pick up your puppy from the breeder for the first time, it is wise to know if the puppy is being served to follow the food to feeding routine. If the puppy is too lean or too big or doesn't grow, promptly contact the doctor and ask his opinion on the right food for your puppy.

When selecting the right diet for your dog, you'll need a full-bodied and nutritious food that's easy to consume and tastes amazing, of course. There are several choices and it can be difficult to make a decision but it can be made simpler by taking your puppy to the Decent Pets and Gardens shop. Our department has completed holistic research on all quality dog diets and should be able to help you with your puppy's best decision.

Take him to some Decent Pets and Gardens to weigh your puppy, and use the exclusive "doggy scales" available in-store. Dry foods are popular with dog owners as they are easy to transport, easy to serve and their crunchiness helps keep the teeth of the dog healthy. Some enjoy adding in hot, processed food that's not required for a healthy diet that can add a little variety.

Puppy biscuits can also be mildly flavored with warm water which can make them more tasteful and harder for baby teeth to chew.

How well to do is solely based on the puppy's age, temperament and activity level, refer to the maps on the dog food packages as they should provide instructions on the quantities to be served.

Where a range such as "feed between 1 and 1½ cups" is given, first start with the lower amount (1 cup) and slowly increase the amount as needed, It would discourage too much feeding and end up with a "tubby puppy"

Young puppies have smaller stomachs and can not eat the requirements of a full day in a single feed so start with three small meals a day. Lower feeds slowly to one in the morning and one in the evening, and make sure to follow the routine. When a puppy gets closer to maturity he reduces the calories he needs, and he can continue to put some food in the dish. That doesn't mean he dislikes the food or is unwell, it's just a indication that he's full and you should only start that his meals a little.

The physiology of a puppy is different from yours, and what could be healthy for you could cause dangers for him. Prevent the existence of small bones, chocolate, milk goods, fat trimmings and sugar treats.

Avoid any major adjustments to the puppy's diet until a doctor recommends. A puppy should have finished developing at between 12 and 18 months and now is the time to turn to adult milk. Any large breed puppies may require up to two years to keep on a puppy diet.

Gradually incorporate the new food over a span of 7 to 10 days by increasing the ratio of fresh food to old food per day. Loose stools or disturbed tummies are a indication the transformation is slowing.

Puppies often chew their own stools. This is not linked to diet but is a behavior that occurs in many dogs through fatigue, lack of activity or even observing this behaviour. It's hard to avoid this but a professional might be willing to provide some guidance. At the very least, pick up any droppings and eliminate the potential as early as possible.

Like other animals, dogs require water to help control their body temperature, eat food, eliminate waste and let nutrients flow through the body. Clean drinking water will still be open to dogs so it's smart to have many containers both inside and out of the property. Make sure they can't be tipped down because it will be disgusting for your dog to be on a hot day without water.

Puppies love to play and this is the best way for him to bond, exercise and grow his energy with you. There is a wide variety of toys available that encourage a puppy to race, play, chew and cuddle and there's unlimited possibilities for fun.
Stop playing with your dog right before bedtime or they'll be full of excitement when you leave home much like a kid who don't want to calm down.
Puppies will enjoy some time quietly, playing alone. Place them in a quiet environment while on their own and give them a range of puppy-friendly toys and chew toys that will keep them occupied.

There are plenty of fun toys online, such as healing balls that hold a puppy entertained while they attempt to roll around the ball and make the treatments fall out. Change the toys every few weeks so the puppy won't get tired and test the toys regularly to make sure they're safe and won't get too tiny for the growing puppy's mouth.

Stuffed toys for children are not appropriate for dogs, as their chewing can loosen and choke on the padding, buttons or loose bits.
Avoid the desire to wrestle with puppies, play "war tag" or games involving scratching or attack. It can be adorable when he's young, but his teeth can become very sharp and you won't want him to stick playing it rough games when he grows up. When he bites, say "No" at the same time as making a quick clap and walk away afterwards.

Sleeping

Sleeping

You may be tempted to make your puppy sleep in your own pillow, but it's important to remember it's a routine that's going to last a lifetime. If you're satisfied when he sleeps while he's an adult, this isn't an problem, but it may be better to find other choices when he's still small. This may sleep next to your bed, in another room, or maybe even under a sheltered patio as he grows older.

Decide where your puppy will be sleeping until you go shopping for a bed. Dog bedding comes with several different features to match your puppy's height, age, and living arrangements.

There are very pretty and functional beds available to match most homes 'decor and have a cozy place to sleep for your puppy. Particularly useful are those with washable tops, so select one that has plenty of padding to provide good field insulation.

When puppies sleep on concrete or frozen floors, some beds are lifted off the floor which is fine. Make sure your dog has a comfortable blanket in his room, or one of your old jumpers, and maybe his favorite toy to cuddle with.

Getting puppies used to brushing early in life makes treating them much safer as they get older. Start out with brief sessions, softly brush their ears and paws and give them a "massage" with your fingertips. They'll be starting to love the focus early and this time together is a perfect way to test for fleas, bruises and cuts.
Gradually implement brushes though they may initially assume this is a toy.

If that's the case, remain cool and use positive reinforcement to praise them with just a few good seconds. Do not raise your voice or get upset at your pet so that they can come to love the experience and not feel nervous the next time they have to be groomed.

Puppies should be bathed even when they're very muddy because over-bathing strips the skin from the natural oils. Choose a shampoo appropriate for the puppy. These are much better than a human shampoo and for a puppy may not have the right pH. Before gathering the puppy for the wash, get it ready- multiple blankets, a blanket, luke warm water and a shampoo.

Place a rubber pad in the toilet or sink to keep him from falling. Blow through some knots before putting water on his shirt. Rub in the shampoo with particular attention to keeping the suds away from his eyes and ear canal and then scrub all around the ears, paws and underbelly. A second shampoo may be required, depending on the puppy's hair. Use a chamois towel to absorb extra moisture, then dry with a soft fluffy towel.

Get a copy of our "Grooming Cats and Dogs" information sheet from the Best Pets and Gardens shop or by visiting our website to find out more about shaving, cutting hair, brushing teeth, ears and eyes and can grooming equipment to use.

Teaching Potty is better than simply getting out your dog every few hours. This needs you to monitor the environment and lifestyle of the dog so that he has no risk of incidents. "Safety Is the Key The secret to potty training is to take the young puppy out regularly (on average for an eight-week-old puppy every two hours) and never allow her the ability to have a potty accident. That is at least eight journeys a day!

To stop allowing your dog the chance to poop indoors, while she's in the house she will either be either

- In her crate
- In a puppy-safe and potty-safe playpen with a potty area that includes a suitable potty surface (such as artificial grass or pee pads)
- Tied to you by a rope so that she can't walk around to potty in the house or under your strict control in an enclosed space. Clear observation ensures you are still staring at her. She'll have a potty mistake the minute you move aside.

Stick true to this program for a month and she will regularly cultivate the habit of going outside and keeping it in. Then continue to keep a close watch on her for a few more months, particularly when you take her on trips to other people's homes, before calling her fully qualified potty.

Potty training starts by learning to enjoy and to sleep in a cage (or other tiny surroundings).

The aim of crate training is for your puppy to learn to enjoy resting in her crate.

CRATE

During the evening, the dog will sleep during her crate and take naps in it during the day. You should make it cozy with a blanket and teach her and enjoy her cage, and put treats inside at odd times. Then send her toys and pet her until you shut the door, while she is in it. The main aim of crate training is to go into the crate by yourself or when you give her a visual prompt, rather than being pushed or coaxed into it. Then once she's in, she's still silent, relaxed then cool.

CRATE SIZE

The crate would be large enough for the puppy to lay down and turn but not large enough for a specific potty area. By inserting a box in it, you can make the crate bigger, and by using a bigger cage, as the puppy grows, expand the crate.

CRATES AND WHINING

The bulk of puppies moan the first time that they're crated. We aren't used to making their families limited entry. It's crucial that puppies understand that being isolated or contained is good, the moaning will end after a week if you're vigilant with the crate training early on. If you reward your puppy by letting her out barking, the barking may become a severe fear or anger obstacle that keeps you from being able to leave your dog alone in another room or in the building.

- Stop letting dogs out of their cabinets while they're barking or moaning, otherwise you're going to encourage the barking / crying activity and it'll get worse. Instead, wait to let them out until they are calm.
- You should even praise your dog for good actions by tossing cookies in her crate when she's still or by opening the door and paying attention when she's silent.
- Make sure to place toys and any of your puppy's meal in the crate if you bring it in such that it becomes correlated with good encounters in the crate
- When you are uncertain if the amount of whining becomes natural, contact an animal behaviour expert urgently until whining is a expensive and disruptive problem.
- Some excellent breeders teach their puppies to enjoy living alone in a cage long before they adopt them out. See how your breeder can continue the crate preparation, how possible, before you pick up your puppy to take her home.

This includes a daily routine and a fast photo of getting Puppy to her Potty Spot. First thing in the morning: Race her to her potty spot as you let your dog out of her crate before she gets a chance to sit and pee. If you're not confident she can keep it outside for long enough to make it, take it out.

Run her out to her potty spot: if you take her out without a lead, walk briskly or sprint down the hall to stop her. She may need to be on leash and she has no chance to escape. Only a one-second delay would give her the chance to sit and get potty inside. That means if you have stairs, it's best to carry her, because her reluctance is enough to encourage her to squat and pee right before the first step.

Wait around while she potsties: Keep her out on a leash so she can't roam and get confused, or better bring her out in a small enclosed area. Silently wait until she is potty. When she is, please thank her, stroke her or give her a treat when she ends. Only look out so you don't stop her from ending. If she doesn't potty after five minutes, bring her in her crate for 15 minutes and then try again. Repeat the 20-minute treatment until it pans out. You should play with her until she's pottyed.

Note: At first, it can be boring. Try listening to music or a book on tape while you're waiting, and even getting a timer so that you don't get restless just for the five minutes.

Start an eight-week-old puppy every two hours. During the day and during the night, eight-week-old puppies will be crated for up to two hours while they are unconscious. Generally, dogs should be crated in months at the same amount of hours as their age during the day. Of starters, if she hasn't had a big drink of water right before going in, a three-month-old puppy will be crated three hours at a time.

Taking her out after a nap: taking the puppy out, in addition to a two-hour rule, anytime she gets up from sleep or comes out of her crate or playpen first

After a play session taking her out to potty: if she doesn't go potty, you should put her in her crate for 15 or 30 minutes and then taking her out again

Taking her out as her body language suggests she's looking for a place to pee: it may be discreet to see signs that she's going to go. They usually start sniffing, circling or walking away from the ground.

Take her out 10 to 20 minutes after getting a glass of water. Switch off her water for about an hour before you switch her out for her last potty day outing, so she can get into the night without potting. She will be able to do so seven or eight hours during the night.

Benefit from your mistakes: Clearly a million times a day, dogs have to potty. Learn to anticipate where your puppy is going to have to leave, and avoid injuries. You should benefit from the past any time she has an injury, to stop committing the same mistake again. Potty training is about building up a routine of going to a potty place if the dog wants to go potty and never giving her the opportunity to have an accident inside.

To train potty you have to supervise constantly
If you can tell correctly when she's going to potty, you can add a
word of warning. Tell "go potty" just once in a loud, motivating
voice, just before you know she's going to sit. When you can
pronounce it consistently just a few seconds before she needs to
stand, she'll come to know that "go potty" means she's going to
do # 1 or # 2. Avoid saying the word over and over or it'll all turn
into static for her.

Potty Training Involves continuous supervision Until it is
successful, the dog needs to be supervised personally or tied to
you with a hands-free harness or a chain or a playpen near you.
Alternatively, in a potty-safe and puppy-safe place, she may be
outside. This can help her learn to watch potty when you're not
outside. Yet resist leaving her out for hours at a time
unsupervised. Realize even the young puppies are less capable of
withstanding warm and cold conditions.

 My puppy is tied to me by a leash: this way, and as I move from
place to place, she's still close by. When she's standing next to
me, she's less likely to have a potty incident, because she's still in
my eyes and I can hurry her out.

She is much less likely to get into trouble — chewing unwanted
things, jumping on tables, disturbing the other dog — because
she's under my close control.

She's tied here by rope to furniture near me: I can quickly praise
her from this place for sitting or lying down peacefully, and
ensure that she's not running away to potty or chewing an
unwanted thing.

Be sure that your dog has plenty of treats to keep her
entertained: she will have plenty of treats to snack on anywhere
she is deployed. If she picks offensive things like your shoes or

paper, remove them from her mouth and from her selection, and put one of her puppy-approved things in her mouth. Similar to a two-year-old girl, for her to get the understanding you will have to replicate this toy trade a number of times.

Make sure she's got things to chew on: Lucy's chewing on a puppy-safe chew toy here — a bully stick. For a growing puppy mind an array of toys is important. When Lucy gets down to a small bit that's little enough to swallow whole but large enough to get caught in her esophagus, stomach or intestines, I'll take away the chew toy.

Playpen: The puppy-safe playpen is an alternative to crating while you're out for extended periods of time. It's got its couch, bath, toys and a potty area covered with pee pads. Hopefully, if she can't afford to go outside she'll want to potty on the covers. The goal of a playpen is for the puppy to establish a tolerance for substrates; she'll prefer to keep her bed clean and potty on the surface that's separate from her room.

My puppy's been used to potting in the yard on fake turf, and an indoor turf potting machine might be a perfect substratum to use in her playpen.

What happens without control of the eagle-eyes? Here's what happened when for 20 seconds, I let Lucy walk off lead. She would've had no injuries for the first three days before this incident. I let her walk off leash into a room with me three times on the fourth day. Two of those times she had injuries, even though she had potted outside five minutes ago and was just out of my sight for only 30 seconds. Each second you can not keep an hand on a puppy, because the puppy is tied to you. The puppy will be in her crate any single time, in a playpen, tethered by you, or at a spot where it's safe to go potty.

Attempt to disturb your puppy by making a sharp, guttural "ah."
Don't shout or chastise her. This will only teach her not to potty
before you or to be scared of you. If it scares her, don't even use
the "aa." Whisk up your dog, then.

Get her out there: Run out as soon as possible.

Reward good behaviour: Bring her in a nice potty spot and
reward her with something she wants when she pots. You should
play for her until she's pottyed. So, next time, promise to watch
her more closely.

Clean up: wipe up the incident with a rag or a towel of cloth.
Then wash the mattress or scrub the floor with an enzyme
cleaner to keep the dog from smelling of urine or feces.

What to do with Small Dogs or Puppies that do not enjoy going out on Cold Weather Potty

Few dogs do not want to go outdoors in cold or rainy conditions,
which may pose a obstacle for potty training. This is where it
would also have been helpful if the breeder or early caretaker
had given brief beneficial exposures to cold or rainy conditions
and damp grass or dusty surfaces to the puppies before you
brought home your puppy.

By getting her out into scenarios she can still handle to play in
these settings, you can focus on teaching your dog to be more
accepting of the tougher conditions. Alternatively you can use an
indoor potty device to teach her to potty indoors.

Chapter Three

Puppy Training For His Small House

Does your dog prefer to sleep for a while under the table, on the desk, or on the coat? The dog feels small and safe in the enclosed area because it is probably a nest for them. You can recreate that feeling in the training house and develop a healthy training environment.

Dogs like a small enclosed space for the security they provide. Keeping a dog in a small house is not a "pet-loving" animal. This method of confinement must not be used as a punishment. This is an additional tool that helps define and control animal preferences for small spaces. When performing preventive training, your dog spends time at home when you are not around to set limits.

The home will help you teach your dog what it needs in the right place. Dogs should not make needs in the same places where they sleep. If you leave your dog in a small house while you are not training, the dog will try to catch it until you release it. Your task is to keep a reasonable schedule with lots of opportunities for your pet to meet his needs and play.

How To Choose A House

The home will help you teach your dog what it needs in the right place. Dogs should not make needs in the same places where they sleep. If you leave your dog in a small house while you are not training, the dog will try to catch it until you release it. Your task is to keep a reasonable schedule with lots of opportunities for your pet to meet his needs and play.

If you buy a small house when you are a puppy, you will need a house with a separator that can be moved to expand two different sized houses or interior areas as the puppy grows.

If the dog is undergoing the chewing stage, a blanket or pillow will make the house comfortable. Your small house should be a place where your dog likes to spend time. Do not chew the bed. Some pets never do, some do not. Never use anything that suffocates you in the house.

- Take your dog home under low pressure, not when you go out. Leave the door open so that animals can explore.
- Remove the collar before putting the pet in the house.
- If a puppy is afraid of the noise of a small metal house on a hard floor, you can put a towel or mat under it to muffle the noise.
- Try putting snacks in a small house. It's like a cookie, and you put your dog in it using simple words like "small house" or "enter".
- Bless him and close the door. Then open it for a while.
- As the puppy grows, the amount of time spent is increased in the small house with the door closed.
- Cries out when the door opens. Then your dog will learn to cry more.
- The general rule for determining the time a pet can spend at home is one hour per hour of age. For example, a puppy older than 3 months can stay at home for 4 hours.
- Do not lock the dog for more than eight hours. The dog should not be left there alone doing what it needs or exercising for a long time.
- The longer the dog is trapped the more exercise the dog needs to do every day. A home is a tool that should never be used to avoid training, exercising, or time with your pet.
- Follow regular walk schedules so pets can rest. To keep the ride quiet, always take it to the same place with a belt.

Preventive training teaches dogs in a very simple way what to do. Don't make it happen in the first place!

The idea is simple. Do not leave your dog where it can cause problems. You can use this method to learn allowed activities without learning prohibited activities. Teaching your puppy to bite his toy is easier than telling him to stop biting on your sofa.

If your dog is left unattended and you do something you don't want, he will probably believe they are great because they are enjoying it and no one corrects his behavior . You should not fix the dog after the fact. It has nothing to do with what you did hours, minutes or seconds ago. Undesirable behavior is strengthened every time he repeats it until you catch your dog in action.

PREVENTIVE TRAINING PRACTICE FIRST OF
Everything, plan to spend a lot of time with your dog in the first months and make sure there is a special place for your dog.

This is all about preventive training. It is very simple and, if done correctly, does not allow you to create bad habits, so it is very effective and does not need to be corrected later. In addition, it helps build a strong bond between you and your dog.

• Put your dog in your room and put some chewable toys in another place.

• If the dog is trying to cause a problem, distribute it with a toy and congratulate it when the dog receives it.

• If you are already causing the problem, "No" and steadily interrupt him. . When he stops, either give him a toy and congratulate him on his interest in the toy, or give him an obedience order and congratulate him for keeping it.

• If you can't stay close to him, put your dog in a special place in the house. It may be a garden or a small area equipped for your safety.

What should you do, how should you not do?

• Use the right voice tone to express YES. Practical and natural to order, and bass to show anger, sharper for praise and blessing.

• Don't harm the dog. Dogs and puppies have no concept of being strongly hit or held. They only learn that they can not trust you and that they can not be afraid of you, making their training even harder.

• YES provides a day-to-day incentive for dogs to be able to consume food properly.

• YES, the dog is happy to do the right thing. In the future, this will help you make the right decisions and it will be enjoyable!

Start with your right foot As soon as you bring home your puppy, create a habit of constantly rewarding the right behavior, including when the dog sits or lies quietly, giving compliments, congratulations, honey, and even food croquettes Should. Rewards help puppies learn to behave more easily and lay the foundation for a fun learning experience in the future.

Holidays are a lot of fun for people and also fun for dogs. It is important to consider some safety issues for your next holiday gathering. When you and your family celebrate together, incorporate your dog in a careful and fun way.

food

Many meetings include great meals and someone may be tempted to give your dog a small meal as a festive feast. Do not give dogs "food belonging to people" because they can cause stomach discomfort, cause suffocation, and make it a habit to ask the table all year round. It would be better to show him much love and affection before and after the meal.

ORNAMENTS AND WRAPPERS
Some dogs are known to nibble. Yarns, garlands, ribbons, and other "chews" are attractive to playful dogs, but can cause internal damage if ingested. If you can't supervise your puppy or dog, make sure it is in a safe area. Buy him some appropriate chewable toys as a special surprise for the holidays.

SWEETS
Pets, like people, can be tempted with the rich things of the holidays. Allowing your dog to eat those treats and sweets can cause digestive discomfort. Chocolate is bad for dogs as it contains the obromine, which is toxic to dogs. Make sure you have on hand some favorite treats for your dog, so that he can also enjoy some delicious things.

A holiday is an exciting moment for you, your family and your dog. But keep in mind that it can be stressful for pets. More people, more noise, and daily program changes can scare and confuse them. Having a dog in a celebration is fun, but don't forget to set some restrictions and take precautions to stay happy and healthy during the holidays.

Many people have dogs, but not everyone knows how to do it correctly. If you are serious about how to keep a dog, here are some things you should know. Here are some tips to help dog owners for the first time.

Home

It is important to give your dog a safe living environment. Indoor dogs are close to all kinds of hazards, such as electrical wires and wired objects. Avoid the best dogs possible at home, paying special attention to chemicals that can cause poisoning, such as cleaning products and antifreeze.

You also need to know the different species of shrubs and plants that are toxic to dogs. Having someone near your home is a disaster that will happen. The most toxic plants include tulips, mistletoe and lilies.

Hood

Clearly the dog needs to be fed every day. The quality of the food you eat has a direct impact on your health, both now and in the future. It is not always necessary to pay for the most expensive dog food brands. However, it is important to choose a high-quality brand.

As a general rule, you do not want to give your dog too many kinds of food for humans. Some of them can significantly change the digestive system. Foods such as grapes and chocolate can be fatal to dogs and should be avoided.

Motion

Your dog needs exercise every day. Exercise clearly helps prevent obesity. However, it also provides other benefits such as promoting blood circulation, promoting strong bones, and providing mental stimulation. Running or jogging with your dog is two of the most common ways to meet your daily exercise needs.

If you like walking, you should consider taking your dog. Dogs are good at swimming too. Classes designed for dogs are also suitable for providing exercise.

Cleanliness

When you have a dog, you need to make sure you have time to groom it. To keep your coat in good condition, you need to brush regularly. Long hair varieties need to be prepared more often, especially if the hair is not finished at home.

Don't forget to brush your teeth every day as well as your dog's hair. Dogs can develop oral problems such as periodontal disease and infection, just as they do not pay attention to oral health. Purchase a toothbrush and toothpaste designed for dogs. Do not use anything made for humans.

Pest

Pests like fleas and ticks can make your dog feel very sick because of constant itching. However, some pests can also lead to health problems. Prevent fleas and ticks in a variety of ways, including necklaces, shampoos, powders, and monthly medicines. It is a good idea to take a monthly dose of a worm because it can be a fatal disease that can be easily prevented.

Veterinarian

Dog owners have to investigate for the first time to find a quality vet for their pets. To ensure that your dog is healthy, an appointment with a vet should be made each year. Finding problems as soon as possible increases the chances of handling the problem appropriately. It is recommended that you watch the dog twice a year as the dog grows up.

Keeping a dog is a fun experience. Remember these tips to help your dog friend live a long and healthy life.

Basic level: Stage 1

The first step in the basic level of dog training is to get the dog's desired answer, generalize them at various places and times, associate them with visual and linguistic cues, and eliminate body language Is not to interfere with your signal. To do this, we recommend that you start with the exercises listed below.

Road clicker

The best way to train a dog is by aggressive reinforcement, so the clicker will be your great ally. Get and check the article for details on how to load. Once you know how to control this tool and use it in dog education, you can start working with your dog.

Recognize name

If your dog is a puppy, definitely the first thing you should do is let him recognize his name. To do this, just say your dog's name in a different place or situation and reward or bless him every time he responds to him.

Follow the meal

In general, all dogs tend to keep track of food with their eyes, but if they don't follow, you should practice this exercise and get it. To do this, place a piece of food in your hand or treat, bring it close to the dog's nose, move the food to the right, and click to deliver with a clicker. Do the same exercise left, up, down. If the dog follows it, it is very important that a few seconds elapse between the click and the food offer, associating getting it.

Go to the phone

Your dog will come to you when you call him by his name, but we encourage you to look for another word that indicates he will come to your phone. This exercise is so helpful that it is interesting to start from the very beginning of the basic level of dog training.

Exercising is simple, say "Come", take a say run, place a treat run between your feet, click with the clicker when the animal is facing you, let the dog treat Repeat the process. For better results, you should practice exercising in different rooms of your home. We follow this strategy to attract the attention of the animals without having to say the complete order. For more information, don't miss our article that will teach you step by step to educate your dog to come to the phone.

Caution

What we want to accomplish with this exercise is to make sure that we are still by our side, sometimes the animals stare at us during the walk. In parallel, it is essential to educate the dog to learn to walk together

In order for him to see us and to know us, we need to practice exercise outside during the walk. Bring a clicker, that is the key to success. So whenever your dog looks at you during a walk, click and give him a treat to reinforce behavior. Very easy! Over time, you should stop serving food and bless him.

Let me

In this exercise, we learn to control our dogs themselves, so that they can smell the food from their hands and not throw them on themselves whenever they want to get what they have. To do this, sit on the floor or chair depending on the size of the dog, take a treat, cover with your hand, approach the dog's nose, smell, hold your hand, lick, and prize Do everything you can to get, but don't give it to him. The moment the animal leaves, click on the clicker to give it a snack, regardless of the reason. Repeat the exercise until the dog associates with getting away with what he wants.

At this point, you can introduce the word "leave" to the exercise after showing the animal treat and before putting your hand on the nose. So just issue an order and your dog will leave.

sit down

This order is one of the most basic of dog training and is included in the first stage. Sitting and teaching our dogs helps us in countless situations in everyday life. Because it can tell you how it feels like crossing the road and when visitors are there. Details how to teach a dog to sit.

Basic level: Stage 2

In the second stage of the basic level of training, you need to not only deepen and exercise the exercises you perform in the first stage, but also eliminate body language, eliminate food, and learn how to use other prizes. In this way, you need to continue exercise exercises and gradually eliminate the benefits of replacing them with gestures that draw attention, such as applause, and enthusiastic blessings when you take the right action.

In the case of a "leave" exercise, you need to learn to show food in the palm, ground, or dog food bowl and control its urge to remove food progressively. In any situation. Also, all exercises must be performed in different spaces to provide "distraction", prevent orders, and allow them to be executed at any time.

In addition, practice new exercises.

Lie

Teaching a dog to lie down is very easy. First, order what it feels like. Next, take a snack, let it smell close to the nose, immediately lower your hand towards your forefoot and lie instinctively. At that moment, click to provide a snack. Instead of the dog lying down, follow the food with your eyes, click, carry the candy to the nose, slowly lower your hands and follow the food with your body. Rewards that you can lie down and click to give.

If the dog lays faster after exercising, you will need to enter the "lie down" command while lying down as it relates to the movement.

Look at me

This exercise is really useful to get your dog's attention, especially during walk walk training with you. It's very easy to get it, as soon as the dog sees you in your eyes, sit in front of your dog with your treat with your hand, click with a clicker and treat to it Please give me. Repeat this exercise until you see your dog moving forward. At this point, when your dog sees you, enter the command "look at me" and follow the exercise guidelines.

Basic level: Stage 3

The intention to achieve in the third stage of the basic level of dog training is to increase the duration of response. To do this, you must mentally say the word "thousand" before performing the action and clicking to enhance the action. Gradually, "Sen", "Sen-ichi, Sen-ji", "Sen-ichi, Sen-ji, Thousand" followed by "Sen-go". If the dog cannot wait, say "no" and resume exercise.

In addition to having your dog wait for prizes, you can work on the next new exercise.

Walk without pulling the belt

This exercise is essential to get a quiet, relaxed and peaceful walk. It is recommended that you refer to an article detailing the steps you must follow to teach the dog not to pull the leash.

Welcome people properly

Regardless of whether we are accustomed to accepting visitors, educating dogs so that they don't jump on people and persevere to greetings and welcomes us free from multiple embarrassing situations. Check out an article explaining how to prevent dogs from jumping on people and greet them properly.

Basic level: Stage 4

The fourth step of the basic level of dog training is aimed at maintaining the position during various activities and making the dog react while further increasing the duration of the reaction. In most cases, achieving the desired result is more difficult than in the previous stage. Therefore you must be patient and consistent. Remember that dog education takes time.

At this stage, do not talk about what to do, but take a few steps to keep the dog stationary while walking. To do this, use the "cast" command, move 5 steps and use the "come" command. When it is pointed towards you, click on it lovingly and interpret it as good as long as you lie down while walking. If you do not hold the position, start the exercise again. You can perform different exercises using both "laydown" and "sitdown" sequences.

Due to the difficulty of this stage, we do not recommend introducing new exercises.

Basic level: 5 levels

The final step in the basic level of dog training is to increase the response distance, even if only a few steps. Therefore, you will follow you to your dog without attaching to it.

The exercise is simple. Simply repeat the process that runs in the fourth stage and the number of steps increases. At first it is not easy and your dog will not hold that position throughout your journey. However, with patience, patience, and aggressive reinforcement, you can maintain it for as long as you need it.

Manual Training Signals

Manual signals are easy to teach and learn for most dogs. All you need to get started is a few cookies. There are many ways to teach manual signals. One of these methods is as follows:
The first thing to do is to associate the dog's gesture with an oral command. Below are some of them. From there, it is a recurring problem.

Suppose your dog already knows the link between the verbal order ("sitting") and the action you want him to perform (sitting). Here we need to create a new association between the unknown manual signal, the word order, and the behavior that the animal already knows. First, associate the verbal order with the manual signal (see below for common manual signal examples). If the dog performs the correct action, use cookies to enhance this behavior. You need to repeat this as many times as necessary to make sure the pet understands the association.

Gradually remove the verbal order while still using cookies. For a while, you can use word order and gesture order in half the time, and use only gesture order.

When your pet learns to react to just the order of gestures by giving a cookie, begin to delete that cookie gradually. Soon, your dog will sit, lie down, and approach the movement of the hand.

SIT
Start with a dog standing in front of you. Hold the cookie in your hand and bend your arm slowly at the elbow to throw something. Do it slowly, pass the cookie near the dog's nose and say "sit" at the same time. Ask him to lift his nose the moment you say "sit". If he feels, bless him and give him cookies.
Laying
Start with a dog sitting in front of you, raise your hand over your head, hold a cookie, and then lower your hand with your arms extended until you come to your side. Slowly, put the cookie through the dog's nose and say "cast" at the same time. The moment you say "Cast", he drops his nose. If he is placed, bless him and give him cookies.
Still
You started teaching to sit on a puppy, but he makes it longer and in most cases only wins prizes. Now you have to train him to stay in one place.

When you feel a pet, put your hand in front of his face and give him the order "Max, Keep".
• Turn slowly and walk in front of him.
• When the puppy wakes up, return to the "sitting" order.
• After a few seconds, bless him calmly and say "good". Please raise it.
• Repeat until the pet remains seated.

• Then go back one or two times. If you follow, start over and gradually increase the distance.
• Repeat until the pet is sitting a few steps while sitting.
• Don't forget to bless her, but keep calm. Too much enthusiasm excites her and makes her hard to keep sitting.
approach
Start with a dog standing in front of you. Extend one arm to the side and hold the cookie with one hand parallel to the floor. Put your arm forward and bring your hand close to the opposite shoulder. Slowly at first, pass the cookie through the dog's nose and at the same time say "here" and take several steps. When the dog approaches, congratulate him and give him a cookie.

Regular Program For Your Dog

Since dogs are ordinary animals, the program is very important. You need to schedule when to feed the dog, exercise, or let the dog download.

Reason for scheduling

The program brings happiness to your pet and gives you peace of mind knowing what is going to happen and when. The curriculum also supports the care and treatment of animals. Generally a curriculum of guidance and support supports the educational process for dogs to learn and meet their needs in the right place.

FEEDING PROGRAM

Give the dog the same amount of food at the same time every day. Give at least once a day. After fifteen minutes, remove any food you did not eat. Always discard fresh water freely.

Knowing what your dog is going to eat and drink will allow you to decide when to stop. We're also learning in digestion. It removes the need of learning to meet your needs.

DOWNLOAD THE PROGRAM

Don't forget preventive training: it is always better to anticipate. If you think a dog needs to unload instead of waiting for a long time to risk an accident in the house, go out with the dog. The more times your dog unloads where you want it, the lower the chance of an accident in the house. The more clear the situation is for a dog, the faster it will absorb what you want. The dog really wants to please you and you can show them how to do it.

Always accompany your dog when he leaves. In this way, you can go to the pre-selected area and remove the habit of searching the entire location and finding the destination area. You will also be given the opportunity to make sure that the dog has been unloaded and blessed before entering the house.

SCHEDULE PUPPY DOWNLOADS

Puppies need to go out frequently. At 8 weeks of age, going out every 2-3 hours during the day is recommended. 4 months is approximately every 4 or 5 hours. Most puppies can spend the whole night without going out in about 4 months. The dog is about nine months old and can get used to traveling three or four times a day, but the higher the number, the better.

PRACTICE AND PLAY THE PROGRAM

Exercise is important for all dogs. Many adult dogs are overweight due to excessive feeding and / or lack of exercise programs. Without proper exercise, dogs may be bored or try to consume excess energy, which can cause them to bite destructively. Let your dog walk for 15-20 minutes a week to help you get to know him. You will have the opportunity to strengthen your bond with the dog.

Train A Puppy - Things To Consider!

Many new dog owners are certainly seeing themselves in love with an adorable puppy. Everyone knows how cute and attractive a puppy is. But sometimes your pet loves you but can bother you. While he is too young, you need to start training the puppy to understand what it should be. Here are some things to know about pet training:

You must establish your position as an alpha dog. Dogs are packed animals, so there are always leaders that other dogs are looking for. Your pet should see you as an alpha dog or its leader. At a young stage, puppies always try to learn from their owners what is right or wrong. Strict pets can be difficult. However, it is good to train pets. Not only does it teach good manners to puppies, it will probably promote a longer and healthier life. Therefore, it is very important that pets undergo obedience training.

Your puppy does not have the ability to understand your language. The breed cannot understand all the words you speak. Therefore, getting a dog to understand your meaning depends on how you teach your dog. Unfortunately, for a puppy, he does not have the ability to understand what he means by the tone and behavior of his actions.

In that case, don't worry when the puppy doesn't react as you want. He did not find even a puppy who did not have enough time to react to the suggestions given to him by the tone of the owner's voice and his actions. So if your little friend doesn't react as you want, you have to put up.

Start puppy training right away. Start training your puppy from the first day you have a dog. While training your pet, you will find that well-behaved dogs will reward you for all your training efforts and that it is great to be with him, the importance of efficient submission training Please make sure you are aware of.

Regardless of age, every dog has very short memories. If you accidentally re blame the animal, the end result possible is that it becomes a badly educated neurotic dog. For example, a pet can do two things about poop.

When there is little education, you can go to a hidden place when you have to go. Or you can eat feces to avoid punishment from you. Therefore, you must be really careful when it comes to teaching puppies. Consider these things to achieve success when teaching puppies sometimes what it should be.

Chapter Five
Train A Dog Correctly To Learn

Partner training needs to be done constantly, this means you need to run your training job continuously and patiently three or four times a week. After a long walk with the dog, you need to start the session.

There is no doubt that the dog has been relieved, ran, played and met the needs before starting a training session (Doberman or Pit-bull). Dogs that are not adventurous simply do not concentrate and do not learn correctly.

To run a training session, you need to choose a quiet location. Other dogs don't get in the way of us, hear loud noises, and people don't always pass. Privacy is necessary for pets to learn and concentrate as much as possible.

Prizes must be prepared to reward the dog for successful exercise. Dog biscuits, sausages and bread are perfect prizes. Mime and love are also good prizes that complement the prizes in the form of food.

PRIZES FOR EDUCATING DOGS
We bless your enthusiasm when our dogs exercise well. good! well done! This is how this is done! Very good Toby! Etc. We reward you with cookies or sausages and love you. He must know that we are happy.

If the dog makes a mistake, he returns to his original position and resumes exercise. If you get to the part where you made a mistake, we will give you a firm voice. Disagreeable! You don't have to scream or punish him, nor give him a prize.

A training session must not last longer than 30 minutes. If you exceed 30 minutes, you will need to play back at least 15 minutes before resuming the training session. Do not exceed the daily training time.

This article will not teach you how to use a dog for self-defense. It is an unnecessary risk for an inexperienced person to teach a dog such a dangerous exercise. If you want to teach dog self-defense movements, you should go to a professional trainer, yes or yes. You should have no reason for doing this. If you accidentally teach a dog a defense movement, it will be a catastrophe.

In a training session, only one order needs to be exercised until he learns correctly. You can't teach him 1000 things, not two things in a single session.
We must always use the same order for each exercise, if one day we teach you to sit with the "Sit" order, we cannot change it the next day or the following week to "Sit down", we must always keep the same orders.

Training sessions should take place in a suitable climate, without too much cold or heat.

Once followed all the guidelines discussed above and located in a quiet place to start the training session, we will see how to teach our dog to sit.

We will not place in front of our dog, with the left hand we will hold it gently by the collar, with the sole intention of not leaving and staying by our side. With the right hand we will press on his back, at the height of the ass, so that he folds his hind legs and feels. While we press with the right hand and he sits down, we will tell him in a firm voice only once the order we want for that exercise, for example "Sit" or "Sit".

When he feels, we will release him and congratulate him, we will give him a prize (cookie or piece of sausage) and we will caress a little. We must repeat this exercise constantly until our dog feels just by listening to the order, when we say "Sit" or "Sit" he should do it alone, without the need to press him on the back with his right hand.

It is not a simple job, we may need a few days to get it done effectively. It is important that on days when there is no training, we repeat this order at home for example, before giving him dinner or caressing him. It is a positive and indirect way to remind you of what we have done in the training session.

As the days go by, he will only do the exercise, then it is time to perform the next step: That they remain seated until we give you the order to get up.

We will perform the sitting exercise with the order of "Sit" or "Sit" and when the dog has sat down, we will gradually move away from him, without turning his back. When he gets up to go to us, we will joke with the "No!" Order and tell him that he feels again.

We must repeat this step until he sits and we can move away from it a couple of meters, without him getting up. We will do it progressively, we will ask you to feel and we will move away half a meter, we will ask you to come with the "Come" or "Here" order to approach us and we will reward you, congratulate and caress you. When you learn to do this well, we will repeat moving away a little more, like a meter. When it does well, we will move away a meter and a half and so on until we learn to sit still even if we move away five or ten meters.

The correct accomplishment of this exercise can take several weeks, especially in breeds a little stubborn as Pitbulldogs , you have to be patient and persevering. Perform the exercises calmly and if our dog does not learn to do it well, it is not because of him, but surely we are not giving him the instructions correctly.

How To Teach Our Dog To Lie Down In A Few Steps

To teach our dog to lie down, we must first have taught him to sit down, this is important in the accomplishment of this exercise.

We will give our dog the order to sit down and when he has sat down, we will take a prize with his hand and put it near his mouth but without being able to take it. Without getting up, we will withdraw the prize so that he leans forward, at the same time we will lower it, so that it also tilts down. With the other hand we will be giving a very soft touch, some small touches on the front legs, so that it stretches forward and lies down.

While you are lying down, we will give you the order to lie down, just seeing: "Lie down" or "Lie down" will be enough. When he has lay down we will give him the prize and congratulate him for having done his job well. Before repeating the exercise we must ask you to get up completely and start from the beginning, give the order to sit down and repeat the process.

We will repeat the exercise as many times and weeks as necessary, until the solo is laid down with the corresponding "Lie down" order. When you do it correctly, we will do the same process we did with the order to sit down, we will move away progressively without letting it get up until we tell you.

The correct completion of this exercise will also take several weeks, you have to be patient and constant. We must never press our dog or stress it, we must not force him to do what he does not want to do. If one day you decide that you don't want to learn, it is best to continue training another day.

How To Teach Our Dog To Walk By Our Side
We will need to tie our dog with a short leash, no more than a meter long. We will begin to walk in the area dedicated to training with care that our dog never tries to go ahead of us. When you try, we will take a 180º turn so that we take a new direction, this will disorient you a little by making you aware of us.

We will take medium-strong rides, turning 90º or 180º unexpectedly. If our dog tries to go ahead of us, we will take a turn so that he has to vary and loosen the leash to follow us. You can see all the techniques recommended in our publication How to teach your dog to walk .

This type of training is possibly one of the most complicated, many dogs have a hard time to walk properly, but when they get it, it is a real pleasure to walk with them. If we see that our dog is too euphoric or that we cannot master the walk, we must use the tricks outlined in the article recommended above.

There are also special "anti-pull" harnesses, which will facilitate this training task if our dog is excessively euphoric.

How To Teach Our Dog To Come To Our Call
This technique is one of the simplest, is to fool our beloved pets with prizes, it is really simple. When our dog is a little away from us, we will get a prize and hold it with his hand for him to see, while we call him and give him the order to come.

It is not enough to call him by his name, but we must give him the order to come, for example if he is called "Tobby", we must show him the prize and tell him loudly to hear us "Tobby come!" Or "Tobby here!" . As soon as he sees the prize he will come running, when he is at our side we will give him the prize and congratulate him with enthusiasm. If our dog sees us and does not come, he does not like the prize you are giving him ... Try a small piece of sausage, they usually like it a lot.

We must practice this technique for several weeks, after this time, we will give you a prize only in an interleaved way, so that when we call you sometimes you have a prize and sometimes not.

Although always, we must always congratulate you when you come to our side in fulfilling the order, over time we can withdraw the prizes completely in this exercise but we must always congratulate you.

Puppies do not need to be trained, because they simply just think about playing and having fun. It is only after five or six months, when we can begin to train them little by little and in a very soft and playful way. We must never force or stress them. The ideal age to start training a dog is from one year of age, in a smooth and progressive way.

Puppies only need to play and run, interact and socialize with other dogs and little else ... let them be happy, there will be time to learn. However, when you see them doing something wrong like biting people (they will play it evidently), you can joke with the "No!" Order so they begin to learn little by little.

Training a puppy is like trying to teach a baby algebra, it makes no sense. Remember, be happy with your little boy and don't be in a hurry to see him grow, everything comes in time

Chapter Six
Canine Training Criteria

Canine training criteria and good ways to succeed by teaching your hairy pet basic dog obedience exercises through positive reinforcement, here you will get some basic guidelines that will help you a lot when it comes to training your dog, both in simple exercises and in other more complicated training processes.

Canine training criteria and good ways to succeed by teaching your hairy pet basic dog obedience exercises through positive reinforcement .

Here are some basic guidelines that will help you a lot when it comes to training your dog , both in simple exercises and in other more complicated training processes . Be that as it may, you should always follow these recommendations ...

PRECISION IS ESSENTIAL

You always need and use the same voice command for the same exercise . If you train your beloved pet to go where you are under the voice command "come here" and next week you say "come here doggy" and the next month you choose to say "come", because in the end your dog will go crazy and he will not listen to you. And not for bad if not because if you change the voice commands of the exercises you learn and then change them you will not recognize those new words with the exercise that you enchanted. You understand?

Another very common example is when we walk with our dog on the street. If we have trained the animal to walk by our side with its harness or collar, since we follow our step but then, for no reason we jerk the dog in full swing, you will confuse your pet.

So you know, be precise.

Reward with many pampering

If something is clear is that canine learning and training will be much more effective and easy to praise and reward with caresses by doing well, and not punishing or yelling at you for doing it wrong . This is very clear. Take it as the first staining of the canine trainer.

The best prize you can give your pet when it does something right is the combination of a small piece of sausage, chuche or canine snack and endless pampering. This is how an animal is trained by positive reinforcement. And do not worry about returning your pet an addict to the sweets, when they learn the exercises you are removing the food prize and in the end they will be content with only your pampering and caresses.

LEARN THE TIMES OF THE AWARDS AND CARESSES

Be very careful with this and reward and thank your dog right after he does the exercise correctly and don't wait . And much less don't give it to him or start giving him prizes for whatever. If you do not realize and give a pet or whatever to your pet when he is doing just something you do not want or dislike, you will be rewarding him for it and will do it again. So let's not use the crazy prizes. Just right after exercising correctly, don't wait.

SHORT AND ENTERTAINING SESSIONS

Exercises and workouts should be fun and not tired or boring. That is why it is best to take it in the best possible mood and use short times in training sessions. Better a 5 o 7 minute session than a 15 minute session . That way your dog won't get bored. And let a good time pass before an upcoming session. And never more than 3 or 4 sessions in a day.

BEWARE OF DISTRACTIONS

To start if you have never trained your dog, start the sessions in a quiet place away from distractions. If you start with the first training and basic obedience exercises and do it in the park near your home, where noise and traffic, along with the barking of the other dogs in the park just make you annoy, it is not the best place to start You are having a hard time getting started. It is best to start your first training sessions at home.

LET'S NOT LOSE CALM OR PATIENCE

If you are in a bad mood and pissed off for anything, or have had a bad day, better leave the dog training for tomorrow . And much less if you start screaming and pushing your pet. You will end up getting afraid of routines and exercises and you will get nothing more than a traumatized dog. And is that ...

YOU CAN ALWAYS GO TO A PROFESSIONAL

If your dog is one of those who resist and do not want to learn, or it is you who do not have free time to do so, it is best to be helped by a professional trainer through operant conditioning techniques . Basic obedience exercises are not expensive and will be great. In addition, in these places of professional canine training, dogs socialize very well, especially with other dogs. Thing that on the other hand will always come with pearls.

KEEP TRAINING AND PRACTICING

The fact is that if you do not insist again from time to time and repeat the exercises, over time, the dog may end up forgetting the older ones. That is why I recommend that you repeat everything you have learned regularly and with new exercises. For example every month at least once. So your dog will never forget what he has learned and will always respond to you with the behavior you want him to do under your order.

A dog's behavior is the biggest trait of his personality, and it is moldable! Never forget this.

You must be constant and patient, and reward your dog for doing well and never shout or punish him.

Remember that you can train a dog at any age, it is never too late. Now, I also tell you that the sooner you start, the better and easier it will be.

Relaxation Exercises For Dogs

the relaxation exercises for very active and restless dogs that have a hard time stopping and going to sleep. Sometimes stress and anxiety usually generate problems when resting. We are going to tell you three excellent ways to relax your pet on the way to bed.

Certainly, some very active pets need you to help them out at night when they go to bed. My greyhound without going any further is one of those bitches that costs. That's why I take advantage when I can to play with my pet and we do training and exercises at night to spend the most of his energies and stimulate him mentally .

And the ideal in these cases is to implement routines in the form of calm techniques for the transition between energy play and training , and bedtime. Creating routines of this type in your pet's regular life is very healthy and can help your dog know when it's time for bed.

Here is a great and calm techniques that are going to do very well when facing a dog that gets stubborn at night when you have to go to bed.

The first thing to keep in mind before starting any canine relaxation technique is to take things easy. Find a quiet and quiet place, keep all your toys and possible distractions. and use a calm and calm tone of voice. Don't you think of screaming or making excessive fuss or your pet will get nervous, or worse, it will be believed that you want to play with her and she will get more excited.

You will also have to be very attentive to the body language and behavior of your pet. There are no two identical dogs and you will have to analyze their behavior if they follow your instructions and are comfortable or feel uncomfortable. So you can assess which relaxation technique is best for your dear canine friend.

Long massages on the sides of the face and body

In general, the best way to relax a dog and encourage him to sleep is through massages and caresses.

So to start with this technique massage the side of the face with soft and slow movements or small circular movements.

You should also treat them with gentle massages throughout the body. As? Well, when you start, place the palm of your hand at the base of your pet's neck and run it down the spine towards the base of the tail. Without squeezing a lot. Just slide your hand several times along your body down the back as if it were in "slow motion" do you understand? L fter again face as the start and finish slowly massaged and loosely at the base of the head and tail.

EAR MASSAGE

It seems silly but dogs ears have a lot of nerve endings, and if
you give massages in the ears can release endorphins in the
body of your beloved pet. I already tell you that ear massages are
one of the best canine anti-stress remedies . They usually work
very well and are very simple to perform.

As? Then start by giving light circular massages with your
fingers without squeezing. And see how your dog reacts to see
how much he likes and if he enjoys. And I told you before that
it's about trying two or three times with each of these three
relaxation techniques and deciding on the one that best suits
your great canine friend.

CHEST MASSAGES

Another very simple technique. It's about massaging your dog's
chest with light circular massages . And do not go over, since
these massages if you do them very fast or strong, generate the
opposite effect. so you know: light and uncured circular massage
on the chest.

Last tips

Then there are specific cases of pets that are working, or practice
many dog sports and develop a great activity. In addition to
using these three relaxation techniques, these dogs will have to
massage other specific areas of their body and specific muscle
groups where the greatest wear is concentrated . For example, if
your pet spends the day running or exercises through speed
races often, you also have to massage his paws, as they wear out
a lot in his daily activities.

Another different issue is if you have injuries, trauma, or very sore muscles from excessive exercise. In these specific cases you will have to talk to the veterinarian.

- The dog is going to believe you have effective leadership over him. To be a good leader is to give structure and direction to your pet. You may think the routine is boring, but it helps your dog understand the world, feel calm, and stay away from issues. Here are some suggestions:• Be kind and respectful when you communicate with your dog.
- •Learn how to control your dog's ears. If he bites you or puts pressure on his muzzle, he will respond with a stern "No Biting!" which will show you that you are not another dog and you should be treated differently.
- • Order "Sit" or "Down" from petting to tossing a toy at him before giving him what he wants. He will start waiting for you to set the rules as he responds to you before you respond to him and at the same time he will get his daily practice of learning.
- • Take the hands, mouth and legs of your dog kindly so you can learn to accept this activity. It begins when you're very young and for a short time. Stay relaxed in the course of these exercises. make them a game. Congratulate it and reward it with treats. These exercises do not present difficulty in most dogs but if your dog struggles and is disturbed, consult your veterinarian or seek advice with a qualified trainer as soon as possible.
- Use different voice tones to communicate different messages. A sharper tone than normal is exciting and fun, perfect for compliments and congratulations. A normal tone, direct and safe, is your tone to Issuance of orders. A lower voice tone is a warning, as it is associated with a

growl by the dog. With practice, your dog can learn
through your tone of voice to understand your mood.

- Recall that with practice and repetition dogs learn. Please
  be patient! If you're doing this way with consistency, your
  dog will become a friendly, well-balanced companion
  with good manners.

Tips To Teach A Dog To Do His Needs In One Place

Before explaining how to teach a dog to go to the bathroom, it
will be essential to take a few preliminary steps and take into
account some basic tips, if not, this process will not work. Keep
them in mind and apply them all :

The corral for dogs : it is a delimited space in which we will leave
our dog when we leave home and it will also be the place chosen
to do their needs. It must be a large space (it can even be a
room) and it is very important to choose a quiet area of the
house without traffic. For example, the hall or hall will not be
good places, we better use a room or dining room.

Hours of urination : usually the puppy usually urinates upon
waking, after eating and after exercising or intense play. Those
will be the ideal moments to bring you closer to your area and
allow you to urinate there.

Always follow the same routines : regularity avoids stress
and helps your dog understand better. Therefore, if you always
follow the same meal and game schedule, your dog will probably
learn to urinate in the right place before.

Avoid punishment and reward successes : it is essential to understand that we can never scold a puppy for doing his needs in the wrong place, we must remember that the mistake is ours for not anticipating or anticipating that he will do so. On the contrary we will always reward the successes, in this way we will achieve that you remember better.

Eliminate prohibited bathrooms: When the puppy makes his needs in a wrong place, there are smells of urine and feces that will motivate him to do so again. This behavior is natural in dogs, and usually lengthens the training time to go to the bathroom. Eliminate those odors and apply a dog repellent made with natural ingredients.

Go to the veterinarian : the puppy needs to receive his first vaccines over 3 months of life, for that reason and taking advantage of the visit to the specialist, it will be essential to consult with him all our doubts and rule out any health problems that are complicating this learning.

Clean thoroughly : yes, never use products such as bleach or ammonia, it is preferable to use enzymatic products.

If you follow these tips you will rule out any health problems in your puppy and encourage him to learn to urinate in the newspaper much faster.

HOW TO TEACH A PUPPY TO PEE IN A NEWSPAPER

Preparing the puppy enclosure

Once you have a puppy enclosure, cover it with a newspaper. Also remember that there are other options that are not newspapers. For example, on the market, you can find "dog soap", a special towel for the floor that absorbs odors. Artificial grass and other products can also be used.

Note that the puppy enclosure should be large enough so that no excrement or urine is near the food dish or home. Unless you can supervise him, your dog must be in that room. Of course you have to leave some toys (big, can't be swallowed) to bite. Also, if you need a meal while you are out, leave a dish.

As time goes on, you will find that your puppy prefers several places to do his needs. If you notice this, you can start shrinking the wallpaper area.

Identify the moment the puppy wants to urinate

It's normal for your puppy to make his needs at the same time, but if not, there are physical signs that we can identify, which will help teach the dog to go to the toilet:

- Walking very fast and nervous
- Sniff the ground
- Walk in a circle

Others cry and look at their owners with a sad face ... Training your dog also means learning to understand the language of the dog. If you know you are approaching time or see signs, take your dog to the selected area and go to the place you need.

If you take him on time and let the urine not disturb him, wait until he finishes blessing him, whether it is by treat, love s or kind words As long as you use positive everything goes reinforcement

START SHRINKING THE NEWSPAPER AREA

Over several days, you will learn to identify your puppy's favorite area to urinate with his dog pen. First, remove some newspapers from where your dog is farthest from dirty things.

In other words, if your dog gets dirty at the bottom, remove the documents from the entrance.

Next, remove the newspaper every day, but don't rush it. If your dog is polluting a place that is not wallpaper, it is because you deleted the paper very quickly. In that case, change the wallpaper on a larger surface or even the entire room.

Once your dog gets used to doing it in a small area, you can start moving documents to where you want. Move slowly to the selected location within 3 cm per day. Do not put documents in bed or water or food containers. If you do, your dog will stop making his needs in the paperwork.

WHAT HAPPENS IF THE PUPPY DOES NOT LEARN

If for some reason the puppy cannot be taught to go to the toilet and therefore does not meet his needs in the marked area, do not worry, and do not quarrel first, he deliberately Don't do it Re-wall the entire area and start the process from the beginning.

Please note that if it is less than 6 months, it cannot be controlled for a long time. Some dogs don't do it until birth. Also, don't let your dog go anywhere in the house. You should always leave him in the puppy park.

WHAT HAPPENS IF I PUNISH MY DOG AND NOW HE IS AFRAID

Some owners take the dog's nose to debris or dirty paper as a punishment method. Apart from the fact that it is not advisable to do this at all, doing it will not help your dog to understand more deeply, on the contrary, your dog is afraid of his attitude and his Impedes possible learning. This method also makes puppies rely on dung food, eat dung and lick their urine, mainly afraid of being prop again.

It completely avoids the punishment of the life of puppies and adult dogs and bets on teaching based on positive methods and rewards. Because research is the best way to learn and remember them. If you punish a puppy and he is afraid of you, try to regain his confidence not only by rewarding him whenever there is an opportunity, but also by doing new exercises, games and activities.

ELIMINATE FORBIDDEN TOILETS AND TEACH DOGS WHERE THEY NEED THEM

Accidents always occur during the training phase. Puppies may be needed where they are not needed. It is recommended to apply a dog repellent to prevent odor during urination and to motivate the excrement to urinate again in this area.

THE NEWSPAPER CANNOT REPLACE THE PARK

It is important to note that having an area for puppies to learn how to do what they need at home cannot replace a walk anyway. As soon as the dog is out (you must first be at home for the vaccine), you must learn how to teach the puppy to walk down the street. Setting the area at home is a temporary solution until the puppy learns to control his bladder.

Making the dog aware of its name is essential for the dog to respond correctly to our signals. It is basic training that allows you to train obedience training for other dogs and draw attention in a variety of situations. If you can't get the dog's attention, you can't teach the dog to exercise. Therefore, it is convenient that this is the first training exercise for dog submission.

Here you will see how to choose a good name, attract the dog's attention, and extend the dog's attention. It also provides useful advice to actively respond in different situations where you can find yourself.

Remember that teaching dogs to recognize their name is a very important task for their owners to consider. All this helps to strengthen your bonds, prevent park leaks and create the foundation for your submission level.

CHOOSE AN APPROPRIATE NAME

It is essential to choose an appropriate name for your dog. You need to know that overly long names that are difficult to pronounce or names that can be confused with other orders should be discarded immediately.

Your dog must have a special and beautiful name, but can be easily associated at the same time. Expert Animal provides a complete list of original dog names or a list of dog short names. It is very important to keep this detail in mind.

Catch the dog's attention

Our first purpose is to get the dog's attention. With this criterion you will try to achieve basic behavior. That means the dog will see you for a moment. I don't need to see you, but I'm careful to make it easier for you to communicate with him after saying his name. However, most dogs will see their eyes.

If your dog is a furry breed and his fur covers his eyes, you don't know where he really is looking. In this case, even if you don't know if the dog is actually doing it, the standard is that the dog points your face in your direction as if you were looking at you with your eyes.

To pay attention to your dogs, we use appetizing food whether they are Go, Run, Skuck, or a bit of Frankfurt. Show him some food, then close your hands to protect the food. Wait with your fist.

Your dog tries to eat food in different ways. He will strike your hand with your feet, lick your hand, whisper to you or do something else. Ignore all these actions and keep your hands closed. If the dog hits you or pushes your hand hard, leave it tucked in your thigh. Use this method to avoid moving your hands.

At some point, the dog is fed up with trying to perform a non-functional behavior. Pronounce his name and when he sees you bless him with "very good" or click (ring a clicker) and give him food.

If your dog doesn't seem to associate the process properly, you don't need to worry during the first iteration. It is normal. Repeat this exercise, click or admire with care, and respond to that name by looking at you. It is important not to reward you if you do not do it properly.

Repeat as necessary

It depends on the dog's mental ability to learn sooner or later in order to correctly associate the dog's name with the awards received later. Don't worry if you don't seem to understand it, some dogs need up to 40 repetitions, while 10 are enough for others.

Ideally, repeat this exercise every day for 5-10 minutes. If you prolong the training session, your dog will be out of tune.

On the other hand, it emphasizes the importance of training in a quiet place where there is no distraction, so that the dog can concentrate fully on us.

Extend the dog's attention

This procedure is very similar to the procedure detailed in the previous point with the goal of increasing the duration of the operation up to 3 seconds. Repeat the previous exercise a few times to start the first session of this standard and allow the dog to participate in the game.

The next step (like the previous process) gets a treat, closes with a fist, pronounces the name and waits. Count three seconds and click or bless him and feed him food. If the dog keeps an eye, you can move and try again so that the dog keeps you focused. It will probably follow you.

He performs the same procedure again, but is waiting for a short time before rewarding him. Gradually increase the time the dog sees in front of the eye until it takes at least 3 seconds in 5 consecutive iterations.

Do as many sessions as necessary until the dog sees the eye for 3 consecutive seconds for 5 consecutive times. The duration continues for these repetitions, even if it exceeds 3 seconds. The intention is to pay attention to the time that the dog will extend your instructions to a minimum.

As I said before, the ideal is not to overwhelm the dog, so there is little training time, but you have concentration.

CAUTION OF MOVING DOG

In general, dogs tend to pay more attention to us when we are moving, but not everyone reacts in the same way. Once our dog sees us, associate a snack, name, and subsequent prizes, we have to go one step further to pay attention on the move

To easily relate movements, you need to start with a few incremental movements. Start with one or two steps after moving the arm holding the treat.

INCREASE DIFFICULTY

After spending 3-10 days to repeat this exercise, your dog should be able to tell his name to call for your attention. However, it may not function in the house as it does outside.

This is because it is inevitable that a dog in front of different stimuli loses concentration. But this same situation is one where the dog must work actively to react equally well wherever it is. Remember that teaching your dog basic obedience can be a great help for your safety.

As with all learning processes, you need to practice with your dog in various situations that gradually increase the difficulty. You can start practicing the answer in your garden or empty Pipican, but you must gradually teach him where you are busy or distracting.

- Teaching a dog to recognize his name-increasing difficulty

- A problem that could teach your dog to recognize his name

The following problems can occur when teaching dogs to recognize their names:

Dogs hurt their hands when trying to eat food: dogs can bite or beat the hand holding food and hurt the trainer. If your dog hurts you trying to eat food, take a snack from your dog at your shoulder level. If you can't reach the food, the dog can stare at you and begin to strengthen its behavior.

In each iteration, lower your hands a little more until your dog can stretch its arms without trying to get food from your hands. Another option used by some trainers, but I don't like it much, but wear thick gloves that protect your hands from scratches and dog bites. If this issue affects you, it's ideal to review articles about bite suppression.

Your dog is very distracting: If your dog is distracting, it may be because he has eaten recently or the training site is not quiet enough. Train at another location and run the session at another time. You may also want to get a little bit of Frankfurt rather than appetizing for the prizes you offer. If you think the location and schedule are right for you, give your dog a small amount of food before starting the session. As if you were clicking on a clicker, but quickly give 5 pieces of food at the fastest speed and start a training session.

Your dog won't stop staring at you for a moment. If you don't stop your dog staring at you for a moment, it will be difficult to enter orders. To distract your dog and use his name, you can throw food to the ground after each click. In this way, immediately after your dog eats food, you have the opportunity to say his name before he sees you spontaneously. Like sowing seeds.

Teach the dog to recognize his name-a problem that could teach your dog to recognize his name

Notes on using dog names

Do not use your dog's name in vain. Regardless of the situation or reason, if you say the name of the dog without strengthening the behavior when you are looking at you, you will erase the appropriate reaction and your dog will pay attention when you say your name Stop. It is fundamental to reward and congratulate him whenever he actively answers the phone.

HOW TO TRAIN IT USING THE LEASH?

The dog needs to walk comfortably on the leash. From a practical point of view, belt means control and safety. It also means the quality of time for you and your pet.

WHY DO I NEED TO USE A BELT?

There are many reasons why you want your dog to feel comfortable with a leash.

• Do not run away during a walk.

• Can be controlled when excited or upset.

• Learn "here" sequences and other lessons with tools you can use for home training.

• In many urban areas, the use of belts is mandatory in public areas.

• You can take your pet with you at any time.

The first step is to get your dog accustomed to wearing a properly positioned collar, he should feel comfortable and should not be adjusted too much. Don't give up the dog's first upset unless it's too tight. The collar must be worn so that the dog cannot take off. Check regularly to ensure that the two fingers fit between the animal's necks. Be sure to remove the dog when it is at home.

Once your pet is comfortable with the collar, follow the steps below to begin training.

• Wear a leash and let the dog walk with her under your supervision.

• Do not pull the belt or force it out when resisting. Squatting to the dog level, calling with a cheerful voice, offering cookies and toys and inviting.

• Guide your dog to the designated location and do what you need. If you resist, use a toy or cookie or treat it to attract.

• Be free a little and reward when you go in the right direction. Best of all, it will tell you that you have made a good choice.

• Normally, walk with your dog on the left side. Get used to it. Bless him and reward him whenever he stays in that position.

• Stimulate a lot of pets so that they notice when they take a walk. Give him an order and talk to him. have fun!

If necessary, you can teach the order "by foot" by starting the walk. Start walking when the dog is on the left. When you leave or want to go out, say "At my feet" and return to the correct position. If you are behind you, it will reach you.

How To Prevent The Dog From Jumping On People

Especially if those people are children or older . And sometimes our pets are so loving that they live in kisses and greetings to us. Sometimes as visible and close as jumping on us. We tell you in this article why they do it and how to get them to stop doing it.

HOW TO PREVENT THE DOG FROM JUMPING ON PEOPLE

Yes, dogs are very affectionate and are always aware of us, sometimes in excess. But they do not do this to "chinchar", but in nature, dogs greet each other face to face, at the same level of each other. And with us they want to do the same, that's why some end up jumping. It is simply to put his face at the same level as yours .Simple right?

Well, for starters, just say that the fault of all this is ours. Because we allow these behaviors, and sometimes we encourage them to do so. And it is that when they are little they start to do this and since they are such cute puppies, we all laugh at them and see who resists the cute little puppy's face.

And of course, these behaviors at an early age, are inserted into the dog's behavior and then to see who is the clever one who takes it off. We must socialize our dog at an early age and not encourage these situations so that he does not repeat them as an adult. A fun behavior as a child, can become a serious problem of behavior of older.

With the dangers that these jumps can have on children and the elderly.

Solving these behavioral problems go through the correct socialization of puppies and adult training . Through operant conditioning .

First control your dog

You should use training techniques and operant conditioning to deter your pet from jumping to everyone who approaches him. But to start, when your dear canine friend does it again, you have to take some of these measures before you start training the animal:

Put the dog in the transport.

Take it to another room, close the door and leave it only for a while.

Put the necklace on.

With this, you will avoid jumping while learning the right behavior.

TRAIN YOUR PET

When your dog sees your attitude in front of his jumps, he will begin to realize that this behavior, far from being rewarded, does not please you, but this alone will not help. It is best to start training your pet to do something he cannot do when he jumps, such as sitting.

So then, when you teach him not to jump on others, you can order him to feel and it will make things much easier for you. and also add that the whole family should know about your workouts so that while you teach them on the one hand, yours do not continue to allow them to jump on top of them or others and spoil the training.

Training techniques: How to prevent the dog from jumping on people?

We go in steps.

First , look for a family member or friend to help you train your dog so he doesn't jump on people. Your helper must be someone your pet knows and wants to say hello.

Second . Tell your dog what it feels like. That first. If you haven't taught him,

Third . May your assistant approach you and your dog. If your pet makes a threat to jump, the visitor turns around immediately and leaves the room closing the door.

Fourth . Tell your pet what it feels like. and let your assistant come again. Then you will have to repeat this step several times until you see that your beloved pet remains seated as your friend approaches.

Fifth , immediately to see that the animal remains seated while your friend approaches your side, you reward him with some toy or piece of sausage and fill him with kisses and affections.

Then you just have to repeat this in cinjco minutes, three or four times a day and you will see how in a few days you get it.

What if it happens to me in the street with people who cross during their daily walks?

Well, you must handle the situation and train your dog at the same time.

First . Prevent the person who crosses you and your dog from approaching and let him know that you do not want your dog to jump on him.

Second and very important. Give the toy to the person you've found to keep it in his hand.

Third . Make your pet "feel."

Fourth . Let the other person to whom you have given the food prize pet your sitting dog and give him the toy. But only when the animal is sitting.

Fifth . Repeat these exercises in two or three sessions a day until your cute pet learns.

What if the behavioral problem starts when he got home and entered the door?

First . Well then when entering the house if your dog makes a jump jump, turn around quickly and leave the house. Leave the dog inside for a while.

Second . Repeat this as many times as necessary, until your pet realizes that he will only receive your attention. It will not take long that you should not do it, but we will have to help you.

In a few times, we see that your dog does not jump immediately when you get home, if not doubt, just then reward your dog with a toy. And repeat until you learn it in two or three daily sessions.

How To Accustom A Dog To The Muzzle

How to accustom a dog to the muzzle? I tell you how to make him feel calm and relaxed when his mouth is covered. Regardless of whether it is a potentially dangerous dog or not.

How to accustom a dog to the muzzle? I tell you how to make him feel calm and relaxed when his mouth is covered. Regardless of whether it is a potentially dangerous dog or not.

Normally, we need the muzzle when our dear friend goes through some stressful or anxious situation, in the face of disputes with another pet, or because it is a potentially dangerous dog .

What is happening? Well, precisely because they are stressful situations, adding a muzzle to your pet if he is not used to wearing it can make the situation worse, because it is something new and annoying for your dog that adds nerves to the state of anxiety that the animal already carries. You understand?

It is best to accustom your hairy pet to wear a muzzle when necessary and from a young age, so that on the day he needs it he will take it to his liking and relaxed.

Occasionally you will need a muzzle if:

The dog is injured or scared and becomes violent.

If you suffer any traumatic situation.

For being a potentially dangerous dog. (How little I like to use this phrase, when we all know that it is the "bad owners" that generate "bad dogs").

A close friend has a terrier and behaves very well at home until it is his turn to cut his nails. Well, I do not know what mania the animal has to this task because when he sees Luis (my friend) coming with the nail clipper in his hand he refuses. So much that it doesn't let him do it. It also gets "edge" when it hurts going out on the field on the weekend and I try to cure its bruises.

Surely you have heard about it that it is appropriate to carry a muzzle in the first aid kit, right? Well, it is for this reason.

As you can see, it is very interesting to get used to muzzle your pet as soon as possible.

HOW TO ACCUSTOM A DOG TO THE MUZZLE?

As always, it is better to start teaching your dog to go relaxed and quiet with a muzzle from a puppy, but if your pet is an adult, nothing happens, it is never too late if happiness is good. Only it will cost you a little more time.

It would be great if you accustom your dog to the muzzle when you socialize it at a young age .

And for this we will use techniques of positive reinforcement of canine obedience to associate the use of muzzle with something rewarding and rich, in this case sweets or pieces of sausage small snack that your canine pet will love it .

I am going to give you a series of tips so that in a few steps you can accustom your dog to wearing a muzzle. The first thing is to let a day or two pass between each step that I am going to tell you. The best are one to three sessions of the step per day. Never more.And always in a funny, friendly tone and never with screaming.

First step. The approach

We are going to leave the muzzle on the floor next to the dog so that your pet smells and is interested in it. You can get their attention with the muzzle in your hand and immediately leave it on the floor. When the animal does, we gently touch the animal's nose and immediately reward the dog with some delicious snack or snack. Then you take the muzzle and keep it. And repeat this country again . So we will get your pet to relate the muzzle to something positive such as a prize.

Second step. Put a lollipop in the muzzle

The next step is to put a treat inside the muzzle and repeat the previous step but with a prize inside. Easy right? Repeat this step two or three more times.

Third step. Put the muzzle

When our pet has become accustomed without fear to put the snout in the muzzle of the floor to eat the toy, in one of these you go and you put it gently while eating the prize inside. And you take it off in a few seconds. Then repeat this step two or three more times.

Fourth step. It is customary!

Now that you agree to have the muzzle on for a while while eating the prize inside, repeat the exercise but this time leave the muzzle on for a minute or two. And at the same time you give him prizes (one every fifteen seconds through the muzzle and with the post. And you take it off. Repeat twice more.

Fifth step and end

Then it is only a matter of repeating this exercise every day and go lengthening the time that your dog is wearing the muzzle and decrease the prizes to one every thirty seconds, then every minute, until he gets used to take it indefinitely as long as we want .

That if, during all the steps, praise your dog for the good that it does and fill it with pampering.

And that's it

I tell you a series of situations in which it will be interesting for your dog to use a muzzle. And it is that according to the personality of the dog and its age, you still need it on one of these occasions:

- Administration of injections vaccines or medications.
- When traveling.
- With the daily walks if in them he meets other violent or aggressive dogs.
- Wound and trauma care.
- When he meets other dogs, cats or children.
- Natural disasters.
- In some emergency.
- Ear cleaning eyes or nail cutting.

And your pet? Do you put the muzzle from time to time?

Puppies from birth have a natural instinct to bite everything they find in their path, since it is in their nature to be able to do so, either for attention, to quench the pruritus of their teeth, to play, to communicate among many other things for which he bites.

It can become a very annoying habit, especially when they have passed the stage of doing so and continue with the problem itself, finding most of your objects, hands, feet, furniture among others, with marks left by having a dog pet.

Among the objects that most attract the attention of puppies are shoes, but they also profess tastes for biting the following:

- Household goods (Furniture and armchairs)
- Toys.
- Teddies.
- TV controls
- Cables.
- Others.

PREVENT YOUR PUPPY FROM BITING

The main thing is to recognize that you have finished with everything you have at home, the clothes, shoes, accessories that are within your reach, becoming a rather big nuisance when you want to reprimand it, because pets are like the children.

Arm yourself with patience, take a deep breath and relax it can become a worse case if you do not teach him that they are small to not bite what is in their way, so it is important that you have some tips and tools that provide you with ideas so that Your puppy stop biting .

Therefore, keep reading that we give you several options so that you stay calm and sure that your puppy will not continue to mess with everything you do, leaving you with broken or broken marks on every thing he uses as a toy to bite . You want to know more?

TEACH HIM NOT TO BITE HIS HANDS

When your pet is a puppy, it usually changes teeth quickly, but unlike the human it does not usually last long, but the sensations are quite similar, especially the itching or itching that occurs in the gums at the time of the teething process .

Therefore it is an excuse that leaves them the habit of biting everything when they grow up and you have to have enough strength to reprimand him at any time you see him doing that, in addition to teaching him with a positive method, so he does not continue with the same.

Among what can bite is the hand of its owner, which has a voluntary movement that the puppy usually follows and catches his attention, capturing his attention to jump over and bite it, for his hunter instinct that is inherited from his ancestors .

WHAT YOU SHOULD DO TO AVOID BITING YOUR HAND

When you move your hands, at any time you speak and make gestures with them, your puppy will immediately look for them because they provoke him and attract attention as a prey ready to be hunted, which you may like becoming a double-edged sword.

Therefore it is convenient that you do not let it bite and so take into account the following:

Dogs should know how strong or weak they should bite, so you have to prepare them from small to do it without harming.

The bite game is usually seen as a training for your jaw, so little by little you teach him to do it so he doesn't hurt.

Try to complain when he does it in a strong way, so that he knows that it hurts you, so you will be given an opportunity to stop when he feels it is something strong.

You must set limits, so a form of this, you do it with the scream, the expression of simulated pain or simply gestures.

Reprimand him seriously, but without infringing fear, so he knows what respect is with love and patience.

You can choose to leave him alone at some point when you feel that the bite is strong or even growls effusively, keep in mind that he is in a learning stage .

Use toys so you can bite them and direct their attention to them and not your hands, this will also help you not to bite anything from your home or closet.

TEACH HIM NOT TO BITE HIS FEET

Puppies also usually like many feet, especially the part of the fingers that are a bit flashy and playful if you move them repeatedly to get their attention on them, so you should be aware of this when you train so you do not bite.

One of the things that attract the attention of the puppies is the way to move the fingers that are striking as well as the hands, only that they are more within reach because it has them close to their mouth and teeth of course.

So it is also usually seen as a training, but you should not let him do what he wants, or behave badly considering the possibility of training him so that when he does, he knows that it is a game and nothing more than that.

What you should do so you don't bite your feet

Do not move your feet or fingers, so you do not engage in a war to the death with your fingers or feet.

Keep in mind to find another position where you can not locate your feet, and thus feel more uneasy, with this the puppy can look for other things such as its center of attention.

Let him get tired, because if you do not move his feet, it will no longer be fun for him, so he will look for something else to bite or play.

Ignore it, that often makes it go away and lose interest in your feet or fingers.

Take him on a walk to burn energy, this often improves his mood and stops biting his feet.

Teach him not to bite things or accessories

The nerves, the energy, the stress or that is only because you have gone to work are some of the things that can make your furry friend want to bite and end everything he finds in his path, no matter where he is .

In addition, together with the aforementioned situations, it is also usually at the time when the dentition suddenly appears, manifesting various symptoms that make you look where you can lash out to leave your frustration or discomfort.

Many times although it may not seem like the symptoms of teething in dogs can be a way of being sensitive to any situation and leads them to bite everything, including your furniture, so you have to have a little patience during this stage.

TIME IN WHICH THE PET STOPS BITING

Dogs usually stop biting more or less until 7 months of age , but not for that reason they will leave the interest of doing so because at any time and during a game they look for an object that has caught their attention since childhood and bites again.

Even older dogs tend to bite when they remember to play, so it is good to let them remember this stage motivated that they are no longer very active and if this puts them to run and have fun, it can be a good option to exercise and stop sedentary lifestyle Do not you believe it?

The best moments are from the first month of birth, when they begin to explore the world and play with their brothers to bite everything they find even among themselves, having fun without knowing that they are training their jaws, especially those of large race.

The firmness in the voice is what will guarantee you to obey at once, leaving the object aside and of course not to do it again; Ask for opinions about what you owe or not when your puppy is starting to bite to train his jaw.

THE PROCESS OF BITING

When you go to work you should leave everything you can reach or bite away from where you are, so you will not get surprises when you get home, especially unpleasant when you take something very precious and undo it with your teeth because you feel alone.

Many times the process of biting is also associated with loneliness, anxiety, lack of exercise or even hyperactivity . An example of this is in Pit Bull dogs , which tend to be too energetic and if they do not release that energy they tend to bite everything they get in their path.

The most advisable thing is that you do not leave him alone, he seeks a company while you work so that he does not feel abandoned, that can cause him stress at any stage of his life, and more if they are older than they are again like puppies but without much energy .

THE RIDES AND THEIR IMPORTANCE

When a puppy walks, it is taking its energy to be more calm and relaxed, it is important to take him for a walk or leave him in a free environment where he can run, jump and find himself in total freedom of movement, which will guarantee you to keep him calm.

Many times after they go from being a puppy to an adult, they begin to bite on warning again and this is due to the lack of exercises, so you have to take a walk to burn energy, remember that they are very active.

Another way to get him to exercise is when you do it, so if you usually jog in the afternoon or in the morning it is a good idea to take him and make him move, this will guarantee that the dog will calm down and not bite your things .

Another thing that we advise you is to take the veterinarian to see if his behavior is about some mischief due to lack of attention, being left alone or lack of exercises, which will keep you from giving him the best to make him feel good.

Attitude to take into account so as not to bother when they bite

First you must be patient, the dog is intelligent and knows your weaknesses, so do not let him see that he can manipulate you.

You have to train him to stop biting what he finds in his path.

To exercise, a sedentary dog tends to obesity and is the root of any problem, so it deserves to be healthy and full of vitality, but controlled.

It is best to teach him that biting your things is not ideal and for this, keep in mind I will buy your own toys to bite.

Always play with him so that he is always surrounded by love and truly feels it.

A dog must overcome its stages and you must let it burn without any problems under your watchful eye.

Seek the help of a trainer if you have problems so that your dog stops biting everything in its path.

How To Educate A Dog With Positive Reinforcement

When educating a dog, it is very important to know that you have to do it with positive reinforcements . It is the most effective and easy way to educate, in addition to the best for the dog. It is a reward system that will teach the dog to do things well, and above all it will reward him whenever he deserves it. This will make the training a very pleasant and even fun time , so that the dog ends up enjoying while learning . You have to be very patient, and above all, never hit him if he is wrong.

WHAT IS POSITIVE REINFORCEMENT?

The positive reinforcement is, for many, the best way to educate a dog. You can teach anything, from a more complex order such as jumping an obstacle, to a simpler one like sitting. The same happens if you want a dog to stop biting for example, or anything that can occur to us.

Its base is in patience and in knowing that the dog should take the time he needs, avoiding that at any time he feels he must hurry. You should be rewarded when you do things right , without the need to punish him when he is wrong. The positive reinforcement focuses on the dog understanding what things to do , and especially when it does something right.

To do this, when training a dog with positive reinforcements, you must have a prize. It is normal to start with a toy, alternating from time to time with some caress or just nice words. The reality is that there are a number of different awards that will fulfill the same function in this type of training. In fact, it is so popular that specific devices have even come on the market.

Educating the dog through positive reinforcements will be very pleasant and effective , as long as it is taken into account that there is no reason to be in a hurry. It is better to educate the dog since he is a puppy, because in this way he will remember all his life what he has been taught at that stage.

What prizes to use

Dogs tend to like sweets a lot , so to start you will have to have one of your favorites . You will be told what you have to do, and if you do, you may be given the kick. However, when you want to try to get a dog to learn many things, it is not advisable to be constantly stuffing it with sweets. For that, little by little you must understand that there are other things that are also a prize , such as caresses or beautiful words. In addition, many prefer to use the clicker for dogs , a device that emits a sound at the press of a button.The dog will gradually learn that hearing that sound means that he has done things well , so he will learn to act correctly.

Of course, there are other options instead of those mentioned. The most important thing is that whatever is done, the dog should know what it means that he has done well what he has been asked. Many act similarly to the clicker, emitting some sound like a simple snap of fingers. It may be equally effective, but there may be problems if the dog hears it in some other context, as it can be confused. There are also similar options for deaf dogs , such as a laser pointer that is activated when the dog has correctly done what it has been asked to do.

BENEFITS OF POSITIVE REINFORCEMENT

Educating a dog through positive reinforcement will make everyone enjoy the training, and anyone can do it without the need for previous experience. This means that normally everyone trains their own dog , which makes them enjoy spending time together.

In addition to learning new things, the dog can also have fun , since he will like to please his human and be told how well he does things. Therefore, educating a dog in this way implies doing new activities with him, which can make the relationship even stronger.

In addition, if that were not enough, through this type of training a dog can learn anything. It is very important to take it into account and apply it in any situation, whatever the dog wants to learn. It will always be necessary to put aside the negative reinforcements , because they will not do any good to anyone.

In recent years, many studies have shown that this type of training is the most effective , especially since dogs learn orders correctly. It may be a bit slow at first, and it needs a lot of patience , but the results it brings without any doubt make positive reinforcements worthwhile when educating a dog.

WHAT TO DO IF THE DOG DOES NOT OBEY

It is normal for the dog not to obey when he is beginning to be educated, especially since he still does not understand what he is told. In these cases, do not despair or get angry, because if the dog notices it could end up stressed. A stressful situation in training could end up leading to a refusal to learn in the dog. It is very important that you understand that there is no hurry and that if nothing happens if you are wrong or do not understand what you are told.

As time goes by and you are being trained, you will obey much more easily. We must make the learning process enjoyable for everyone , which implies understanding the dog's needs and that can also be mistaken from time to time. In fact, it is something that will happen very frequently at the beginning so it will be better to be clear before starting any training. Above all, you should never shout or hit him if he is wrong.

NEVER USE NEGATIVE REINFORCEMENT

Negative reinforcement implies that the dog learns anything based on fear. This means that you will not be rewarded when you do something right, but you will be punished when you make a mistake and do not do what you are asked to do correctly. As expected, this type of training makes the dog afraid to learn, as it relates to a punishment and, therefore, to have a bad time. As if that were not enough, for many the punishment is not simply to scold the dog, but also to beat him. This should not be done under any circumstances, and it is absolutely useless.

The dog will have a bad time unnecessarily , and although he seems to obey quickly, he will do it with great fear of being punished. You will not understand the orders correctly, which makes it very easy for you to get even more confused as you learn new things.

Training based on negative reinforcements is not at all effective , and you always have to remember that dogs are friends and more family members , so on no occasion will you have to hit them. As the most important thing when educating a dog is to be patient , it is clear that you should not lose it if you are wrong, and always understand that you must take the time you need to learn.

How To Teach To Walk To Your Puppy

When you go for a walk your puppy , there is a different way for each breed or way to train your dog that show those people who have a dog in their lives, so a big dog is different the way to walk it to a small one for what it is important to know how to walk it.

The hairy people have the need to sniff the way they go, the people they cross, the places they pass through and even make a travel itinerary so they learn to walk later without a leash, free and without getting lost or running from side of the master.

The highlight of all this is the possibility that you teach him to walk without having to pull the belt, drag you or be he who takes the reins of the ride and so be happy both the owner and the furry friend, being that he wishes is Go out to stretch your legs and make your needs.

A constant fight, the belt

For dogs there is a rather difficult problem when it comes to going for a walk, and it is that it bothers them many times to have to wear a collar or harness and the chorea with which they should be subject to you. Is that the first problem presented? Of course yes.

So much so that you have to accustom it at home to put on the necklace and leave it for a moment to feel it on your neck, in order to get used to it little by little, taking into account the age, size and date on which The dog has reached your hands.

Do not force him to anything if you feel he feels imprisoned, put on his collar and leash when he feels that he is familiar with the two objects, and does not growl at him, he feels scared or he may bite you if he feels threatened by this.

Keep the following in mind when it comes to finding the special collar and leash for your dog :

The size of the collar, while the first should be between 120 cm or 130 cm, leaving a thick finger between the neck and the collar on the dog.

Some necklaces should have lights when it comes to walking them at night and if you let go of the strap, to avoid losing it.

The thinner leash for small dogs is better, the big ones must of course be thicker and firmer when you have to pull it.

The strap should have a length of 100 cm to 130 cm too, so you can give it space to walk freely.

Let him sniff everything in peace and when he stops, let him feel the ground.

Rehearse with short walks for a reasonable time

First of all it is advisable to take him on trips that do not tire him much, always waiting for the possibility that he will get used to the itinerary chosen for him, taking advantage of every moment allowing him to recognize the terrain.

As you progress, the path of the ride will increase, leaving space for a week to progressively increase the ride and with a specific time between half an hour to an hour first once a day, then two and end with three daily walks .

This may change as you have become accustomed, taking into account the itinerary also the stipulated time in addition to the times you take it for a walk, remembering not to force you to do something that you are not prepared or have done before.

STEPS TO START TAKING YOUR PET FOR A WALK

Call him and show him the leash and the collar, so that he gets used to it, that is the signal to walk .

Put the collar and the strap on slowly to accept it without nervousness or fright.

After that, open the door slowly, so that you become aware that the meaning of all this is the way out.

Always walk next to him and fit your way of walking, if you feel you want to move forward, do a further stopping the step, until you realize the meaning of stopping or following.

Reinforce your learning with a prize , as instructed by the canine training manual in positive, with a dog biscuit or other form.

Return to the house and take off the leash and collar, after that you have the possibility to play with your pet for a while and flatter him for how well he has behaved.

Over time, think about removing the leash while walking.

THE PUPPY AND THE WALKS

The puppy is always more active, energetic and eager to enjoy the outdoors, especially if you have kept it within the home for a reasonable time, but it is also the easiest to handle, teach and for being young you have the possibility to learn faster .

When you take him out for a walk, keep his temper in mind , since outside the home he becomes nervous as well as quite anxious; It is important to teach him the activities with which later you will see positive results when making the dog obey everything.

The puppy has the possibility of being easier to teach, so you can also give him his prize every time he behaves well and shows that he has learned his work very well, always reinforces his learning with a feasible teaching.

THE PHYSIOLOGICAL NEEDS OF PETS

The dog has the possibility to learn to do his physiological needs from the first walk, generating a routine that you must keep at the same time, the same times a day so that the dog can learn that the walk also means let off steam.

It is feasible to be offered gifts and prizes as learning progresses, especially at times when you take a positive action that requires you to be congratulated, making the special moment between the two of you when you receive the prize for good behavior.

In addition to all this, it is an important option to have the double possibility where your dog rests its sphincters when venting in addition to excreting the waste that the body does not need, helping him to stay healthy, healthy, happy and at all times loved.

THE DAILY WALK

What does the walk bring to your dog daily ? Get your basic needs to be solved, feel happy as the walk progresses, pay attention to the person you love, stay alert as well as being linked to you at all times with love and dedication.

The time you have to have it for him at all times, so follow the schedule without changing it so that you do not confuse it and have problems with your needs, also remember that it is a human being that needs attention just like you at all times and is a Huge responsibility to have a dog.

In addition to all that, the daily walk will give you stress , throw away the energy you have in excess, provide exercise as well as play, offering you happiness while getting used to a routine that gives you reasons to worship as your owner.

What you should not do to walk your dog

Do not force your dog to do what he does not want, that can bring you behavioral problems, disappointing both your furry friend and you.

Do not force him to take a different behavior than what you have taught, that can also bring you little affective behavior.

Do not forget to always give the prizes, even after having achieved the learning.

Encourage your dog to enjoy the walk by walking, stopping, and following the path in this way will help you later to not need the leashes.

To learn to walk your dog you have to feel like doing it and be patient, keep this in mind.

Try to obey all orders without a joke and if you see that he ignores you, ignore him and get away from him immediately.

AVOID BARKING OTHER DOGS

During the first days it is normal for dogs to bark at others of the same species, in addition to growling, it is important to keep this in mind, since they usually bark at each other to mark territory, teach him who commands besides defending what belongs to them .

In the latter case you have the option of being yourself who is part of your property, therefore you should take into account what happens to them normally, avoiding at all times that they do so after having socialized with other dogs .

On the other hand, as you walk, you have the possibility of forgetting your surroundings to play, exercise, do your physiological needs among many other activities with which you can be distracted, it is usually an option to make you forget of everything to calm down.

THE WALK A PUNISHMENT OR A REWARD

Do not try to punish him when not making an order as you asked, remember that they are like children and learning is a bit more tedious because they do not know how to talk, but if they communicate, then treat it as if it were one of your children .

It is important that you encourage him when they fail to make an order, that can scare them by causing them to be prohibited from doing so, so it is necessary that you rebuke him with love, but at the same time with firmness they will understand that if they do something well they receive a prize or positive reinforcement , but should do better.

THE COMMUNICATION OF THE DOGS

Believe it or not they can communicate with you, reading many times the expressions of your face in addition to your mood, remember not to mistreat him when he is asking you to leave it is important to remember that he is waiting for that moment to let off steam.

Also that when you take him out for a walk, it is possible that some bad gesture that you do during the journey can cause nervousness, fear and uncertainty, achieving with these feelings that run away from you and you can lose sight of it, be careful with that.

The best thing is that both of you are relaxed and use that walk to relieve you of stress, clear your mind and play with each other that reinforce the bonds of friendship, trust and love existing between you two, improving your mood and changing your condition. physiological

PATIENCE AND LOVE

So that you do not have problems with your hairy, we emphasize the fact that you are at all times patient and calm, especially if you can not do any of the learning activities that you have imposed during the hours of walking, that is not achieved quickly.

How To Educate A Puppy That Bites To Stop

I think it's great that you play a lot with your dog, but when you do it be careful and do it from the beginning having soft toys that you can bite so that when your puppy "pulls" to bite (I insist that it is normal behavior in a puppy) instead of your hands, you bring a toy to your mouth to bite it. Easy right? You will see that he soon gets used to this and leaves your hands and ankles calm.

Another training and canine exercise technique to solve the problem is to do the following: Try to do this. When your puppy is going to bite your hand, you give him a voice command, the one you want but in an energetic way, something like "still" or "for". Whatever, but always the same word. So the animal will go back a few moments and you take your hand from its reach. You immediately stop playing with your dog for a few minutes and you don't pay attention to him.

Soon, play again with your dog but this time he uses his toys with your hands, so he doesn't bite you, and when he does it as you want, at the moment you reward him with some "chuche" that he likes. That is, we use operant conditioning techniques , (clicker type) with prizes. And it's just about repeating these new behaviors as I tell you until in a couple of days you'll see how he learns.

NO PUNCHES OR PUNISHMENTS

The fact of shouting loud and angry, punishing your dog or even suppressing those behaviors with blows will not help. What's more, you may make matters worse , while lowering the link between your dog and you. In addition, animals that are punished when trying to repress behaviors often end up retaliating against aggression with us. Better fill your puppy with pampering and affection! This does work.

When you educate or release any dog that does not bite your hands or anyone through the techniques that I have told you, if it does well, in addition to the prize give many caresses and love. This creates on the one hand a real sensation to your dog that he is doing well and also reinforces the owner-pet bond . With what will be easier and easier to teach your puppy new behaviors and to be more obedient. And don't you think of hitting your dog!

Well, I've done everything you tell me and my dog keeps biting me

Ok, this does not change in two minutes and despite everything, until you learn (you just have to be patient, some learn before others) you must continue to insist a few more days. And as with us the pace of learning varies depending on the individual.

If in spite of everything you do not get it and it turns out that your puppy is very "stubborn" and does not want to be right, it is best that you seek professional help and do not leave the problem for tomorrow. The more time passes, and the greater the animal, the more it costs after it learns, so don't leave it.

And do not confuse a behavior with health problems , such as infections or some pathology, or with discomfort in the dentition of dogs when they detach themselves from milk teeth and new and definitive ones come out.

First of all I recommend that when you go to start any series of training with your pet, you are relaxed and do not hurry! It is very important, since the animal will notice any hint of stress or anxiety that you generate on your part and the dog will be more aware of your mood than what you want to teach him. If you feel angry or frustrated at that time, you better leave the exercises with your dog for another day. And is that dogs often perceive these moods right away. And more if they are negative.

1st The first thing you have to do is stand in front of the animal and make it feel . Better if you also feel at their level. If you do not know how to make your dog feel through a voice command, you better wait for your pet to feel at home, take advantage of the moment and stand in front of him.

2nd Then take a piece of sausage or a "chuche" and show it to your furry friend. When you realize that you have the treat then you close your hand so that it cannot be eaten. Always do this in front of him and with your arm extended in front of your head.

3º Move your hand with the prize inside the clenched fist so that the animal is interested in it and wants to eat the candy you have hidden At the same time you say a voice command, the one you want, that if, always the same, as " chócala "so that it associates the command with the action of giving the leg.

Why?

Dogs usually act to this challenge trying to access the inside of your fist with your mouth several times, and will not succeed.

Next, he will try to take the "chuche" that you have stored with his legs. Do you follow me

4th When your dog's paw touches your hand, (believe me he will try) you immediately say "good" (you can also use a clicker , it is easier for him) and then you open your hand and let him eat his prize , that He has done very well.

5th Afterwards it is only a matter of practicing these steps three or four times for two or three days and that's it! In a few times that you continue with the training you will see that your dog offers you the leg when listening to the word you have chosen, even before seeing your hand with the prize inside.

What if my dog gets stuck or ignores me?

Not all dogs are the same, it happens to us, that there are more clever and less ... Well if your pet does not catch it at first (very rare and difficult thing to happen) follow these tips:

If you have tired of practicing these trainings and your dog still ignores you, you will have to facilitate the matter. Shake your hand with the candy inside (step 3) but this time you bring the closed fist in motion to its leg, a span or less. You will see how this time if he listens to you and you get this way that your pet learns to shake hands with the voice of the command you want.

If after all this your furry partner still does not "catch it" you can try the following:

Repeat steps 1, 2 and 3. And then take his leg with your other hand, put it at the height of your clenched fist and shout "well" (or use the clicker) and then reward him with another pooch. Repeat this last step several times and when you master it, return to the original training from the beginning (step 1). You will see how he understands you now and does it well.

Very important...

It is, like almost all workouts, to have patience and repeat several times, all that are necessary. And above all remember that they have to be short sessions, and repeat them three or four times a day. If you do not follow these parameters and you exceed the sessions or their time, your dog will end up getting bored or frustrated. With what you will eventually get nothing. Moreover, if you see that after repeating two or three times the animal loses interest or becomes overwhelmed, for training until the next day.

The key is few short sessions every day. It is a matter of regularity more than anything else. Do not forget to end the sessions by filling your pet with pampering and affection , no matter how well he has done. It's about associating workouts as a positive . It is no use pissing off, getting heavy and repeating to satiety throughout the afternoon. Many less screaming or hitting. Then you will never learn.

And when I stop giving prizes by hand?

This is important. At any given time, you will have to stop teaching your fist with the hidden prize so that it gives you the leg, how? It's simple...

No more "sweets"

A- Show your pet your fist with a hidden prize. (Repeat steps 1, 2 and 3) As soon as you kick, this time you offer the prize but with the other hand NOT WITH THE CLOSED FIST. And repeat this several times.

B- Then you repeat the first three steps again, but this time when you show him the fist with the prize inside and you say "fuck it, let it be an open hand and without a bump, and when you give it a leg you give it a prize with the other hand, as in step A. And now it's just a matter of repeating this several times until you learn it.

C- Well, when you see that your pet has learned well that by saying "chócala" he paws and rewards you, you stop giving him prizes little by little , that is, for example start repeating the exercise three times and only reward him The first time and the last. In a couple of days you only reward him the third time, and in another couple of days you stop doing it, and instead of a food prize, you caress him and give him pampering. You will see how soon he forgets the "sweets" and conforms as a prize with your touch.

And ready. In addition to having a good time and joining more in tune with your pet, it will shake your hand just by saying "chócala" And not only that, your friends and other people who know your dog can also do it. And it is that these training exercises usually work with other people around the animal, once you have taught them.

Taking your dog on a travel requires a bit of thinking, you need to be sure if your dog is ready both physically and mentally, Ask your self in certaintyif the dog can tolerate it, but making it fly for many hours just to stay in their little house once they arrive is not fair to either.

BEFORE TRAVELLING

- Make sure you inquire about how welcome your dog will be in your destination. Cultures are different do not forget that.
- Visit your veterinarian, make sure your vaccinations are up to date and get updated copies of the health records for your trip. It is important that your veterinarian confirm that the dog is in good health for traveling.
- Ensure you know if there is any health issues (that is, insects, cold, heat) at the destination and take the necessary precautions.

PACKING FOR THE TRIP

- Take your dog's health and vaccination certificates against rabies (they are needed when crossing few borders).
- The photo you should use will be the rescent of the dog, for identification if it is lost.
- Put your plate of food, the drinking fountain, the belt, the toys, the little house, the medicines and the cleaning equipment in the suitcase.
- You must bring your food if you travel by car or if you are not sure of getting it at the destination. Sudden dietary

changes can cause digestive disorders and ruin the trip for your pet and youself

- Ensure that your dog has its identification plagues, with your contact written on it and preferably that of the place of destination.

TRAVEL BY LAND

• It's easier to have a doghouse or a dog carrier in your vehicle's rear. Do not expose it to sunlight directly.

• If the dog is out of the carrier, make sure the buckled belt is in place. Special harnesses are attached to the seat belt for sale. If the gear stops suddenly, serious injury could occur, do not use a leash.

• Don't leave your dog in the van's open box.

Do not feed your pet for at least 3 hours before you start your journey.

• Give your dog fresh water to drink during the stops. For being such a good travel companion, you can also reward him with a treat.

• Feed your dog shortly after arriving or stopping for the remainder of the day.

• Wear a leash before you leave the vehicle.

• NEVER leave your pet alone in a closed vehicle. Heat and insufficient air circulation can quickly cause heat stress or even death.

AIR TRAVEL

• When delays and transfers are longer, try to avoid times of increased activity to travel.

• Plan a trip with as few stops and transfers as possible.

• Make your dog's hotel and air bookings well in advance.

• Some airlines permit small dogs to travel with their owners (usually at an additional cost) if the carrier fits under their seat.

Otherwise, rent or purchase a carrier or small house that complies with the airline's regulations and attach an adhesive label with the LIVE ANIMAL legend. Write your name and address and the gender of the person that your dog can contact at the intended location if necessary.

• Place a blanket or pillow at the base of the structure. Add water to the house door with a drinker. The tank is meant to be deep and not too full of water to avoid spillage.

•Take your dog for a long walk on the day of the flight before you leave for the airport.

• At the end of the trip, immediately pick up your pet.

• The dog can spend some time in quarantine in some foreign locations. Find out the country you plan to travel to with your travel agent or consulate on this page.

AT THE DESTINATION

• It complies with all pet regulations at the holiday spot. When you leave your dog alone, leave your dog in a small house, carrier or limited space. Collect your waste quickly. Your consideration is going to help pets stay as guests.

Chapter Eight
What You Should Avoid While Training A Puppy

These are what is NOT to be done during the training, since if we make the mistake of training our pet badly, it will cost us twice or triple to retrain it correctly. Let's see what mistakes we should never make:

- Never shout, scold or hit your dog. Physical or psychological punishment is not effective, it is more than proven and it is cruelty. He would never do it to you.
- Never despair, patience is the mother of all sciences and training a dog takes time, you must have a lot of patience.
- Do not use choking or torture collars, it is an unnecessary cruelty. There are a thousand effective ways to train a dog and none of them is done through punishment or torture.
- Never use different ways to address him, always call him by name and then give him the order.

What To Do During Dog Misbehavior

All dogs make mistakes when they start training. Check the situation and identify the cause. This may be a sign that the dog doesn't know what it can tolerate. As a coach, you need to find and resolve the cause of confusion.

The younger the puppy, the more often it is necessary to evacuate. A 2 month old puppy may need to do it every 2 hours. Physically it can not last more than 8 hours. As the digestive system matures, the interval between defecations increases.

Too much freedom is the most common mistake. Some puppies understand the concept of evacuating outside in weeks or days, but this behavior needs to be strengthened for several months until the pet is 100% reliable. . If your dog meets his needs where he hasn't rented him once or twice, you're likely not monitoring him well.

If you get a small house that is too big for your dog, he will fulfill his needs at one end and sleep at the other end.

Do not hit your pet. Dogs don't understand when they are struck or grabbed. He cannot associate punishment with past mistakes and believes you are angry for no reason. You may be scared and confused.

Changing a dog's diet can cause digestive disorders that can cause accidents. Let me eat at night without evacuating.

Even a well-trained dog may be wrong to meet their needs. Clean the area with an odor neutralizer. That way, pets don't want to make mistakes. Products containing ammonia smell like dog urine and should not be used because they attract them.

If your well-trained dog begins to have accidents, it may be because he does not have enough opportunities to get out and evacuate, also because you are not giving due attention to his signs, or he may have health problems.

Look for territorial brands: small urine traces on various objects. This behavior can be stopped by sterilizing females or males, and diapers are also specially designed for this purpose. Remember to monitor and stop your dog if it starts dialing; then carefully clean the area.

The main thing to keep in mind when educating a dog is that it should be done based on positive reinforcements, giving them some reward for doing things right . You have to allow them to be wrong , because they will feel very confused at the beginning and they should know that this is not bad, that they do not have to be in a hurry to learn.

It is necessary to eliminate, thus, the traditional training based on negative reinforcements , since the dog should never be punished for making mistakes while training, let alone be afraid. In addition, the best way to educate a dog is to start doing it in its puppy stage.

Educate them since they are puppies
Like humans, dogs learn much better in the early stages of their life. They will be much more receptive to orders and their great curiosity for the world they have just arrived will encourage them to learn new things. The puppies are very playful and eager to pay attention, so they will be delighted if they are trained.

An adult dog can also be trained, but if he has not had any education throughout his life, it will be much more complicated. However, with patience, affection, and always making the dog feel comfortable, it will not be impossible. The most important thing is for the dog to enjoy while being educated, and especially to avoid being frustrated or afraid of being punished. This is especially important in adopted dogs, since it is not known what they may have suffered before.

Positive reinforcements
Training based on positive reinforcements is the most efficient that can be found. Not only because the dog will learn any order

correctly, but also because he will enjoy doing it and it will be a fun way for him.

It consists of rewarding the dog when he does what he is asked to do , whether by means of a lollipop, a caress, some pleasant words or something he likes, since it is something that depends a lot on each dog. The important thing is that you learn to relate to do what you are asked to get a benefit , so you will always want to obey your coach, in addition to having fun and wanting to learn new tricks.

Dogs also enjoy when they are told that they have done things well. Therefore, without seeing that when training , nothing happens because they are wrong , but they will receive a prize when they do things right , they will never say no to being trained and able to demonstrate all the things they know how to do.

This type of training, in addition, makes the dog develop a great relationship with its trainer, because they will spend a lot of time together, and learn to enjoy . In addition, the coach is also an important figure in this training, because he must know how to treat the dog with all the love he deserves , never making him feel bad about his mistakes. This type of training is the most effective for any dog , be it pet, police dog or even guide.

Specific objects: The Clicker
Educating a dog with positive reinforcements is so successful today that there have even appeared different devices whose sole function is to participate in this training. An example is the clicker, a small utensil with a button that emits a sound when pressed. The dog will learn to relate that sound to something good, so he will do everything possible to do what he is asked to

listen again. There are those who make a specific sound, without
the need to acquire a clicker, or who use different techniques
such as a laser pointer. They are all equally effective, although it
is essential to be careful and not use them in excessWell, the dog
could be confused.
The clicker must be activated immediately after the order has
been given , so you will know why it has been activated and what
you have to do the next time you are given that order. In
addition, using a sound that is not specific to your training ,
such as a whistle, can make the dog listen to it in other areas and
to other people, which can confuse it.

ELIMINATE NEGATIVE REINFORCEMENTS
Traditional canine training is based on negative reinforcements.
This implies the punishment of a dog when he is wrong, so he
will learn from fear of being punished , and he will never enjoy
learning.

Luckily this type of training is lagging behind, being replaced by
positive reinforcements. However, there are those who claim
that it is very effective , and they do not care how the dog can
feel or make him suffer, and they even have special objects such
as collars that give electric shocks or spikes. This more than
being elements that favor training, they are elements of torture
that will cause the animal to live in a constant fear of being
punished and wrong, eventually rejecting learning. In addition,
excessively mistreated dogs are very likely to become aggressive
to try to prevent them from being harmed again.

While training based on positive reinforcements favors the
connection between the dog and the human, making them enjoy
spending time together, this other training ends up causing the
superiority of the human being to end up scaring the dog , who

will not want to continue learning and, Of course, he will never have a good time.

Training a dog should bring benefits for both of you, both for the trainer from whom the dog obeys orders, and for the dog itself that must enjoy doing things right, never having fear of failure. There is no point in making them have a bad time just so that the human is above them, especially when there are other training methods that are much more effective and that benefit everyone.

RETHINK THE ADVANTAGES OF NEGATIVE REINFORCEMENTS

The defenders of this training are convinced that it is very effective because of how quickly it works, but this is because the dog has learned to be afraid to do things wrong, so he will try to listen to his coach whenever he understand to avoid some punishment.

It is not worth treating a dog to eliminate some training time, especially because he will not learn the orders correctly, becoming confused when he tries to teach more than one, more than anything because he will be spending more time thinking about what can be punished, what you have to do.

HAVE A LOT OF PATIENCE

With a dog, especially if it is a puppy, it is essential to have a lot of patience when teaching new orders, as well as educating them in general. At first it will be difficult, because they will not understand what they are asked for, they will feel confused and sometimes frustrated without knowing very well what to do.

When they begin to understand they will be happier than ever ,
so it is very beneficial for them to understand that there is
nothing wrong with making mistakes or taking time to learn, but
that they have available all the time they need to be taken, and
that based on mistakes they will be able to comply with what
they are asked for.

Therefore, the dog feels that his trainer does not despair , but
has a lot of patience and nothing happens because they take
time to learn , it is something very important when it comes to
educating him .

Otherwise, they would understand that they are a hindrance and
very unintelligent , because they do not understand what they
are asked for and also their coach is angry, so they will not want
to continue learning anything. With patience and making him
feel comfortable, educating a dog will not be complicated.

You allocate the resources!

It is advisable not to give any dog any convenience at all
times. The puppy should not all toys are not always at leisure,
but only be brought out when needed. So you are the one who
decides when the dog is allowed to play and when not. A positive
side effect is that the toy does not lose its appeal.

In addition, you should decide when your puppy is allowed to
eat and when not. It is only allowed to approach the bowl after it
has been released. Limit the time in which the feed is
available. If your dog has not eaten after twenty minutes, take
the bowl away. For older dogs, you can also use the Learn to
Earn method. Your dog must earn his food through performance

and, for example, small onesLearn tricks or perform retrieval exercises with the food dummy.

Educate puppies early

Depending on your domestic circumstances, you can create taboo zones for your puppy and forbid him, for example, to enter the kitchen or the bathroom. The older your puppy gets , the less he should be allowed to follow you every step of the way so that he does not become a control freak. Restrain the movement of the puppy a little so that he does not always and everywhere hangs on you.

In addition, you should teach your puppy table manners, which is part of a good education! To avoid penetrating begging, you should consider a regulation for your own meals. For example, you can ask the dog to stay in place while you eat. This is also very helpful if you go to the restaurant with him.

Chewing on furniture

Most puppies will try it sometime, at the latest when the tooth change is due: chewing on furniture or other objects. If you notice that your dog child is interested in a table leg or similar, interrupt it with a calm but severe stop signal and immediately offer him an alternative to chew on the puppy.

This can be a stable toy or a suitable chewing article such as a buffalo skin bone. So your puppy will quickly learn what he may use for chewing and what not. Also, consider exactly what your protégé may play, because a thoughtless choice can easily cause confusion for him. If he plays with you with an old towel, He probably does not differentiate between a towel and a tablecloth and, in an unobserved moment, clears the coffee table. And if he is allowed to retrieve the slippers, he might think that he can abuse them as chew toys as well.

Prevent feed aggression

A very important point in puppy education is that your puppy gets used to it from the beginning that you give it its food, precisely because there is a risk that he will take up food in the open, which can harm him. Take your pup off and on while he eats the bowl away. But do not overdo it.

If your dog is constantly worried that his food will be taken from him, it will stress him and a food aggression may arise from it. It's quite possible that your dog might come up with the idea of snarling. Do not make the mistake of pulling your hand away at this moment and being intimidated. Then, your puppy gains the learning experience of coming to its destination with aggressive behavior.

Measure it with the necessary rigor short and precise and take the food anyway. The moment your puppy retreats and shows placating behavior (paw, lower tail, put on ears, etc.), praise him in a calm voice. Put his bowl back and give him a chance to do it better again.

In most cases he will not do it again and you can immediately give him back his food bowl as a reward. If your dog growls again, repeat the procedure until he understands that his behavior is unacceptable. Do not worry that your dog might bite you directly if he growls at you.

If he is from a good breedercomes, is healthy and has no "prehistory", is not to go out. The growl is a completely normal and healthy behavior, which he has already tried out with his siblings and initially says only: "Stop that, I do not want that!". By interrupting his threatening gesture, you communicate to him that he is not entitled to show aggressive behavior towards you. However, it is not sensible and even dangerous for a dog to practice this form of communication (ie also when dealing with conspecifics), because this prevents one of the warning signals on the way to a serious attack and trains him without warning.

Conclusion

All dogs deserve good care and don't have to be arduous or costly to train the puppy. If you're sharing your house with a new puppy or an elderly dog, it's never too early to continue your dog training. Most dogs are happy with the stability and trust that comes from the teaching.

Dogs want more than anything to make their owners happy- that's why they train easily. Before you start, make a list of the basic commands you want to teach: "Sitting", "still", "come", "down" or "no" (always useful commands). You can also control the king, teach them not to order food, and avoid accidents in the house. All this can be done-you need consistency, praise, occasional rewards, a lot of patience and positivism.

Be cautious and forward-looking in the event of an accident while teaching a dog to go to the bathroom. This is one of your dog's most important things to teach, starting with a program. Hogs are typical animals, so take them to the toilet after feeding, playing, waking up from a nap, before going to bed or looking for a place to urinate and add these moments into the system.

When the dog is in the right place, laud him a lot. Next time only snacks are going to be motivated. The puppy will learn when and when to do that as time goes on. Remember, it's not all perfect puppies.

When you first start focusing on dog training it can feel daunting. If you're uncertain where to get going, create a week-by-week plan to better organise yourself. Select one or two key commands every week to focus on. Prepare to make any changes to the dog's lifestyle to avoid or change issues with behavior.